EAST LANCASHIRE DERBIES

Blackburn Rovers v. Burnley

Dean Hayes

Published by Sigma Leisure – an imprint of
Sigma Press, 1 South Oak Lane, Wilmslow, Cheshire SK9 6AR, England.

British Library Cataloguing in Publication Data
A CIP record for this book is available from the British Library.

ISBN: 1-85058-759-0

Typesetting and Design by: Sigma Press, Wilmslow, Cheshire.

Cover Design: Belvoir Cartographics

Cover photograph: 27 December, 1976: Burnley's Ian Brennan fires home a late equaliser in the 2-2 draw with Rovers *(Dave Harwood)*

Printed by: MFP Design & Print

Preface

There is no love lost between Blackburn Rovers and Burnley and we have to go back well over 100 years to find the origins of this rivalry. The two clubs first met at Turf Moor on 27 September 1884 with Rovers emerging as winners 4-2. The Clarets didn't have long to wait in gaining revenge, winning 5-1 on the same ground in March 1885. These pre-league friendlies were keenly contested games with considerable pride at stake.

The clubs were among the twelve original members of the Football League and there is no doubt that Rovers were the early masters, completing the 'double' over the Clarets in each of the first three seasons! The first league meeting between the clubs resulted in Rovers winning 7-1 at Turf Moor, a scoreline they repeated on home soil the following season.

The Clarets' first victory in the league came about when Rover's goalkeeper Herbie Arthur was the only player on the pitch, following a snowstorm – the referee decided to abandon the game but awarded the points to Burnley, who lead 3-0 at the time!

The clubs first met in the FA Cup in the quarter-final in March 1913 and Burnley, who were then a Second Division side, beat high-flying Rovers 1-0 at Ewood Park. One of the most memorable FA Cup-ties came in March 1960. Burnley were leading 3-0 but Rovers produced a tremendous fightback to force a replay with three late goals. The second meeting was an ill-tempered affair but Rovers won 2-0 before going all the way to Wembley where they lost to Wolves in the final.

This book, the first-ever written on the meetings of these two famous East Lancashire clubs, contains information on the grounds, every match report (135 matches – League, FA Cup, Test Matches, Anglo-Scottish Cup, Manx Cup and Wartime games), player profiles and an informative statistical section.

Acknowledgements

I would like to express my grateful thanks to the following organisations who helped me in the compilation of this book: Blackburn Rovers Football Club, Burnley Football Club, The Association of Statisticians; staff at the Blackburn and Burnley Central Libraries, the Harris Library, the Lancashire Evening Post and Burnley Express, whose chief photographer, Dave Harwood was especially helpful.

Dean Hayes

Contents

Introduction   1

The Grounds   4

The Matches   8

Star Players   132

Statistics   145
    Blackburn Rovers   145
    Burnley   145
    Biggest Wins   145
    Highest Aggregate Score   145
    Most Appearances (League and Cup)   146
    Most Goals   146
    Four Goals in a Match   146
    Hat-Tricks   147
    Highest Attendances   147
    Select Bibliography   147

Derby days, past and present   148

Players, 1888-2001   155

Introduction

There is no love lost between Blackburn Rovers and Burnley and we have to go back well over 100 years to find the origins of this rivalry.

Blackburn Rovers was founded in 1875 and in the years that followed, the game of football was quickly taken up by the area and such a climate spawned the development of other clubs from local towns. One such club was Burnley Rovers who began life as a rugby club until deciding to change codes in 1882. Calling themselves 'Rovers' wouldn't have gone down too well with the folk of Blackburn but fortunately, the name was soon dropped.

The two clubs first met at Turf Moor on 27 September 1884, with Rovers emerging as winners 4-2. The Clarets didn't have long to wait in gaining revenge, winning 5-1 on the same ground in March 1885. The first meeting on Blackburn's then home ground of Leamington Road ended all-square at 2-2. These pre-League 'friendlies' were keenly contested games with considerable pride at stake. The total number of these pre-League meetings was thirteen, with Burnley winning seven, Rovers four, and two matches being drawn.

The two clubs were among the original twelve members of the Football League and there is no doubt who the masters were, with Rovers completing the 'double' over the Clarets in each of the first three seasons! The first League meeting between the clubs resulted in Rovers winning 7-1 at Turf Moor, a scoreline they repeated on home soil the following season. In that first meeting, Jack Southworth netted Blackburn's first hat-trick in the Football League. The Clarets eventually recorded their first League victory over Rovers in December 1891 when with Burnley 3-0 ahead, Blackburn's Lofthouse and Burnley's Stewart received their marching orders. The rest of Rovers' outfield players went with Lofthouse, leaving goalkeeper Herbie Arthur as the only Blackburn player on the pitch. The referee wisely decided to abandon the game but awarded the points to Burnley!

Rovers though continued to have the better of things in their matches with the Clarets, registering five consecutive wins at Ewood Park in the years just before the turn of the century.

Burnley's greatest moment around this time occurred in the final game of the 1895-96 season when they beat Blackburn 6-0 at Turf Moor with Tom Nicol scoring the first and only hat-trick by a Burnley player against the Rovers in a first-class fixture.

The clubs next met in the Test Match series at the end of the 1897-98 season – a forerunner of the current play-offs, the matches were used to

1

determine the make-up of the First Division for the next season. Rovers had finished next to bottom in the top flight whilst Burnley had won the Second Division Championship after being relegated the previous season. The Clarets won both encounters with Wilf Toman netting a hat-trick in the first match.

The clubs first met in the FA Cup in a quarter-final tie in March 1913. Though Burnley were then a Second Division club, they beat First Division Rovers at Ewood Park 1-0 with Tommy Boyle scoring the all-important winner.

Burnley's relegation at the turn of the century, meant a gap of thirteen years before the two teams met again and then they only enjoyed two seasons in each other's company before the outbreak of the First World War. When the hostilities ended, the East Lancashire Derby came into its own with Blackburn and Burnley meeting each other in the top flight for eleven years in succession.

The Clarets experienced the initial dominance, winning the League Championship in 1920-21 and completing the 'double' over Rovers in successive seasons. The mid-1920s saw three Rovers players – John McIntyre, Arthur Rigby and Ted Harper – score hat-tricks, the latter in his record breaking season of 1925-26 when he netted 43 goals in 37 games.

After Burnley's relegation in 1930, a six-year gap ensued before Rovers, too, lost their top flight status and the teams met for the first time in Division Two in October 1936, playing out a rare goalless draw. In the return match, Rovers winger Jack Bruton scored in a 3-1 win – he remains the only player to have scored for both clubs against the other – having netted twice for the Clarets against Blackburn in the 1920s.

Rovers won the Second Division Championship in 1938-39 and they were joined by Burnley who won promotion in 1946-47, the first season of League football after the Second World War. The Clarets not only consolidated their position in the top flight but finished third, whilst Rovers suffered relegation to the Second Division.

The club's second meeting in the FA Cup was in 1952 when, again, the underdogs came out on top. Second Division Rovers beat First Division Burnley 3-1 at Ewood Park.

It was only after Rovers won promotion to the First Division in 1957-58 that fixtures between the two clubs were resumed after an eleven-year gap. Burnley had the better of these meetings, winning four years in succession at Ewood Park, culminating in the Rovers losing their top-flight status in 1965-66.

Probably the most memorable occasion in the club's FA Cup meetings

2

came in March 1960 when both clubs were in the top flight. Burnley were leading 3-0 with goals from Pilkington, Pointer and Connelly but the Rovers produced a tremendous fightback and after Douglas from the penalty-spot and Dobing had reduced the arrears, Mick McGrath levelled the scores to force a replay. The second meeting at Ewood Park was a rather ill-tempered affair but extra-time goals by Dobing and MacLeod saw Rovers home and they went all the way to Wembley where they lost to Wolverhampton Wanderers.

When the Clarets were relegated in 1970-71, another meeting between the clubs seemed possible but Rovers, too, suffered relegation that season, dropping into the Third Division!

Burnley returned to the First Division a couple of years later but, after being relegated in 1975-76, they met the Rovers again, this time in Division Two, as the Ewood Park club had won promotion in 1974-75. Burnley definitely had the edge, winning four of the six meetings before Rovers went down to Division Three again at the end of the 1978-79 season. Though they bounced back immediately, Burnley were relegated to the Third Division for the first time in their history in 1979-80. The Clarets won promotion at the second time of asking in 1981-82 to set up a renewal of the fixture.

However, much has happened to both clubs since crowd trouble marred their last meeting prior to the 2000-01 derbies, at Ewood Park in April 1983 when the home side won 2-1.

Burnley endured a decline that saw them narrowly escape relegation to the non-League in 1987 when a last-day victory against Orient earned them 90th place in the Football League.

In contrast, Blackburn rose from First Division obscurity to win the Premiership in 1996 thanks to the millions of the late Jack Walker.

The Clarets have waited a long time to meet their neighbours on an equal footing and though passions ran high in the two meetings last season, Rovers' promotion to the premiership means it will be at least two more seasons before the clubs could meet in the League!

The Grounds

Blackburn Rovers' early years saw them use three different pitches including Pleasington Cricket Ground before they settled at Ewood Park. By Christmas 1877 they had rented the Alexandra Meadows where during their two-year stay, they entered the FA Cup for the first time. The club also had a taste of floodlit football in November 1879 when Darwen were the visitors. Darwen were also the opponents twelve months later when an estimated crowd of 10,000 crammed into the ground as well as packing the grandstand, twenty lorries providing raised platforms. Eight minutes into the second half with the scores level at 1-1, a couple of players were involved in a brawl, which resulted in a mass pitch invasion and the abandonment of the game. In February 1881, Alexandra Meadows staged the England v Wales game but at the end of the season, Rovers moved to a new ground at Leamington Street.

Large crowds gathered on 15 October 1881 for the first game at Rovers' new venue, a local derby against Blackburn Olympic, which Rovers won 4-1. The club's first season at Leamington Street was to become their best to date when they reached the FA Cup Final only to lose 1-0 to Old Etonians. The club's stay at Leamington Street lasted nine years, this period representing one of the most successful in the club's history. Their honours included their winning of the FA Cup in three consecutive seasons and their entry in 1888 to the first Football League in the world.

In common with much urban development in industrial Lancashire, Ewood Park was built in the late-Victorian period. Opened in April 1882, it had staged football, athletics and dog-racing among other activities. It was 1890 when Rovers moved into Ewood Park, playing their first match there against Accrington in September of that year. The following Christmas brought crowd trouble. Darwen were the visitors and so incensed were their supporters when Rovers saw fit to field only three first-team players, that they pulled up and broke the goalposts, smashed dressing-room windows and tore up carpets in the reserved seating section.

The new venue was an immediate success. In 1891, England staged an international match against Scotland at Ewood Park whilst an early attempt at floodlit football was made in October 1992, also for a game against Darwen

The ground witnessed further crowd problems during Everton's visit in January 1896 when part of a stand collapsed among a 20,000 crowd. The ground received little attention during the years on either side of 1900, but in 1903, the Darwen End of the ground was covered at a cost of

4

£1,680. The following year saw even greater improvements as the Nuttall Street stand, designed by Archibald Leitch, was built at a cost of £24,000. In between two championship wins in 1912 and 1914, the club built another stand, the double-decker Riverside stand. In 1928, the wooden perimeter railing was replaced by a concrete wall, the Blackburn end was terraced and the Riverside stand re-roofed, for a total outlay of 1,550. A year later Ewood saw its largest crowd – 61,783 for the visit of Bolton Wanderers. In 1958, the club installed floodlights, first used for a friendly against Werder Bremen.

Ewood Park had to adapt more than most grounds to the requirements of the 1975 Safety of Sports Grounds Act. Without this work, it is highly likely that more damage would have been done by a fire that broke out at the Blackburn end of the Nuttall Street stand in July 1984. The club chose a novel way of restoring the damage by building into the stand's existing structure a new block of executive boxes and a glass-fronted lounge overlooking the ground. The development, which cost about £250,000, was named the John Lewis Complex in honour of the club's founder. The Riverside stand was demolished and replaced by a much smaller structure seating around 700 supporters. In the summer of 1989, the pitch was dug up and a revolutionary new surface with under-soil heating was laid.

In 1990, Walker Steel was bought by British Steel for the astonishing sum of £330 million and so, lifelong Rovers' fan Jack Walker who had been born in the back streets of Blackburn, decided he wanted to give something back to the town.

Walker's millions went initially into team building but before long, his plans for rebuilding Ewood were unveiled. The redevelopment plans were finally approved in June 1992. Walker had little difficulty in meeting the council's requirements that he buy up the houses of any residents who wished to sell at 20 per cent above the market value. Demolition of the Nuttall Street houses started in October 1992, prompting all householders to take up Walker's home and away scheme in preference to remaining as the club's neighbours. In March 1993, the Darwen End came down and, at the end of the season, the Blackburn End was cleared along with the houses on Kidder Street. By the start of the 1993-94 season, the lower tier of the new Darwen End was ready, followed by the upper deck in October 1993 and a month later, the lower tier of the Blackburn End. By the time the rest of the Blackburn End opened in February 1994, the Nuttall Street Stand had been flattened. This was replaced by the Jack Walker stand, which was completed in November 1994, leaving Ewood Park with a current capacity of 31,367.

Burnley played their first game at Turf Moor in February 1883, when they entertained Rawtenstall, a match they lost 6-3. Within two years, Burnley had built an 800-seat stand, adapted 'a natural earthwork' to hold 2,000 standing spectators and, at each ended, added uncovered stands for over 5,000 more spectators on wooden benches. They were certainly needed, for in Burnley's first season, over 12,000 crammed into Turf Moor for the visit of Padiham.

In 1886, Turf Moor became the first football ground to be visited by royalty when Prince Albert who was in the town to open a hospital, went to see the Clarets game against Bolton Wanderers, a match the visitors won 4-3.

By 1908, two sides of Turf Moor were covered; the Main Stand on Brunshaw Road and opposite, a structure known as the Star Stand. Around this time, a terrace cover (similar to the Darwen End cover at Ewood Park) was also erected at the Cricket Field End as gates continued to rise.

After the First World War, attendances continued to rise and in February 1924, a record crowd of 54,775 was present for the FA Cup game against Huddersfield Town. Sadly, as in common with crowds of this size at this time, there was widespread crushing and this resulted in one man's death.

The following years saw the lower reaches of the Long Side being properly terraced in concrete, a process which extended up its cinder slopes until in the mid-1950s, the whole bank was covered by a £20,000 roof. Floodlights were installed in December 1957 and switched on for the first time for a friendly match against Blackburn Rovers.

By this time, the Clarets had a new chairman in the shape of Bob Lord. Destined to become one of the game's most controversial chairmen, he engineered the club's ascendancy both on and off the pitch. Completely ignoring his fellow directors, he bought 80 acres of farmland for an advanced training centre at Gawthorpe where the club set up a youth scheme which quickly became the envy of much larger clubs.

Bob Lord was determined to modernise Turf Moor and in the summer of 1967, work began on a £180,000 stand seating 4,500 and housing all the players' 'facilities' at the Cricket Field End.

The stand, which incorporated oil-fired heating for the fans, was eventually opened in 1969 but within two years, the system had to be shut down as it was proving too costly! The Cricket Field Stand was belatedly opened on 23 November 1973 by Bob Lord's personal friend, the Prime Minister Edward Heath. For a while, the Cricket Field Stand became the club's main stand, while the pre-1914 Main Stand was replaced by the new, single-tier Bob Lord Stand. Edward Heath opened this stand on 14 September 1974. At this time, the only uncovered section of the ground was the Bee Hole End, named after a colliery which used to stand behind it.

Though the effects of the 1975 Safety of Sports Ground Act was felt so acutely by other local clubs including Blackburn Rovers, Lord's policy was at least vindicated in terms of subsequent expenditure. For whilst most clubs had their capacities cut drastically, Burnley actually managed to raise theirs! Also, the Clarets' outlay of around £600,000 on safety work between 1977 and 1994 was well below that of comparable clubs.

Since the Taylor Report in 1990, the club has been torn between the need to keep up standards at the ground while not jeopardising the team. As a result of this, plans for a £6.6 million redevelopment of the Long Side and Bee Hole End first drawn up following Burnley being twice promoted between 1992-1994, had to be scaled down when they dropped back to the Second Division in 1995. However, with the offer of a £2.25 million Football Trust grant confirmed in April 1995, the club decided to grasp the nettle.

Contracts for two new stands costing £5.2 million were agreed with a Lincoln building contractor, Linpave. The first task at Turf Moor was to clear the Long Side, the Football League's last great bank of side terracing. This was replaced by the North Stand, which can hold 8,000 spectators on two tiers. The Bee Hole, too, has been replaced by a two-tier stand, leaving Turf Moor's capacity at 22,546.

The Matches

Note: names of scorers are in CAPITAL LETTERS *for ease of reference.*

Match 1
3 November 1888
Burnley 1 Blackburn Rovers 7

Despite the scoreline, it was Rovers 'keeper Herbie Arthur who was forced into making a number of early saves, punching clear from Yates before a shot from Gallacher scraped his right-hand post.

Rovers' first attack ended with Poland saving magnificently from Forrest but the ball had been hit with such ferocity that it burst and had to be replaced! The game was 20 minutes old when FORREST opened the scoring, weaving through the Burnley defence before slipping the ball past Poland. Rovers soon extended their lead through FECITT and then added a third when Jack SOUTHWORTH squeezed the ball home from close-range. The home side pulled a goal back when Yates' cross was met by McKAY, his header giving Arthur no chance. Just before half-time, BERESFORD gave Rovers a 4-1 lead despite the Burnley defence appealing for offside.

The Clarets began the second half with great determination and McKay brought a fine save out of Arthur but, after this initial burst, it was Rovers who made all the running. SOUTHWORTH brought an excellent save out of Poland before eluding a reckless tackle by Bury, he scored Rovers' fifth goal. Two minutes later, Beresford's run and cross down the right led to FECITT scoring from close-in. Burnley's nightmare was complete five minutes from time when SOUTHWORTH got his third and Rovers' seventh to complete the Clarets' biggest home defeat in the East Lancashire Derby. The Clarets almost reduced the arrears in the last minute but Abram's long shot was pushed onto the bar by Herbie Arthur.

Burnley
F. Poland; A. Lang; W. Bury; J. Keenan; D. Friel; J. Abrams; W. McKay; R. McRae; W. McFettridge; J. Yates; P. Gallacher

Blackburn Rovers
H. Arthur; James Southworth; J. Forbes; J. Douglas; W. Almond; J. Forrest; J. Beresford; N. Walton; Jack Southworth; H. Fecitt; W. Townley

Attendance: 3,000

8

Match 2
4 February 1889
Blackburn Rovers 4 Burnley 2

Though Rovers had the wind at their backs and made all the early running, it was their goalkeeper McOwen who was forced into making the game's first real save when he tipped McFettridge's shot over the bar. McKay almost opened the scoring for the visitors but his shot was well held by the Rovers 'keeper.

Rovers took the lead just after the half-hour mark when Jack SOUTHWORTH made a run down the right-wing before cutting inside and hitting a powerful shot out of Cox's reach. The home side extended their lead a couple of minutes later when James Southworth's shot was to strong for Cox to hold and his brother Jack SOUTHWORTH followed up to score his and Rovers' second goal.

Within a minute, Burnley had reduced the arrears when GALLACHER's long-range shot found its way through a crowd of players and past the unsighted McOwen. The Clarets equalised through BRADY who forced the ball home from close range in a goalmouth scramble in which James Southworth was injured and forced to leave the field. These four goals all came in the space of five minutes but there was still time for another with WALTON giving Rovers the lead on the stroke of half-time.

Blackburn's ten men put up a valiant fight in the second half as the Clarets pressed hard for the equaliser. McOwen in the Rovers goal made a number of outstanding saves but then completely against the run of play, TOWNLEY broke away to notch the home side's fourth goal. Towards the end of the game, there was a nasty clash of heads, which resulted in both Douglas of Blackburn and Yates of Burnley having to leave the field for treatment. Though Yates soon returned, Rovers played the last few minutes with nine men and though Gallacher eventually did find the net, his effort was ruled offside.

Blackburn Rovers

W. McOwen; James Southworth; J. Forbes; J. Douglas; W. Almond; J. Barton; R. Haresnape; N. Walton; James Southworth; H. Fecitt; W. Townley

Burnley

W. Cox; A. Lang; W. Bury; J. Keenan; D. Friel; W. McFettridge; W. Brady; A. Brady; P. Gallacher; W. McKay; J. Yates

Attendance: 2,000

Match 3
26 October 1889
Blackburn Rovers 7 Burnley 1

Though Burnley were under strength for this East Lancashire derby with four first team regulars missing, their performance in this meeting at Rovers' Leamington Street ground left much to be desired.

Rovers won the toss and playing with the wind at the backs, spent virtually the whole of the first period camped in Burnley's half of the pitch. They took the lead as early as the fifth minute when William THORNLEY gave Cox no chance from close-in. Further goals from CAMPBELL and WALTON followed before an injury to Townley forced him to withdraw from the game. This didn't deter Rovers and they added further goals from Jack SOUTHWORTH and CAMPBELL before WHITE put through his own goal to give the home side a 6-0 lead at the interval.

Burnley did have a couple of chances to reduce the arrears towards the end of the first half but Friel and Murray both failed with just Arthur to beat.

It was thought that with the wind behind them in the second half, the Clarets would make a much better showing. Even with Rovers centre-half Dewar a passenger on the wing, Burnley still couldn't find a way through the Blackburn defence.

Midway through the second half, Rovers extended their lead when WALTON scored his second goal of the game with a hard, rising shot that left Cox well beaten. With ten minutes left to play, the visitors finally got on the scoresheet when CAMPBELL rose high above the Blackburn defence to head home McFettridge's free-kick.

Blackburn
H. Arthur; T. Brandon; J. Forbes; J. Douglas; G. Dewar; J. Forrest; James Southworth; H. Campbell; Jack Southworth; N. Walton; W. Townley

Burnley
W. Cox; W. Bury; E. White; W. McFettridge; A. Lang; J. Keenan; R. Haresnape; J. Campbell; T. Murray; D. Friel; J. Yates

Attendance: 4,000

Match 4
22 February 1890
Burnley 1 Blackburn Rovers 2

Burnley had shown an improvement in form over recent weeks and so the return match with Blackburn Rovers was eagerly anticipated by Clarets fans.

In fact, the home side took the lead after just three minutes when following good work by Lambie, outside-left STEWART took the ball round Horne before slotting it into an empty net. Lambie was causing the Rovers defence a number of problems and he thought he had extended the Clarets' lead after ten minutes but his powerful strike was disallowed for offside. Burnley continued to push forward but Horne was in brilliant form, saving well from, both Lambie and Hill. When the Rovers 'keeper was beaten, Forbes cleared off the line in spectacular fashion although two minutes later, he almost put through his own goal as his sliced clearance scraped the outside of Horne's left-hand post. Rovers equalised against the run of play when in a rare attack, WALTON fired past Kaye after Townley had missed his kick. Burnley again went in search of further goals and though Haresnape came close, the score at half-time was 1-1.

The visitors thought they had taken the lead in the first minute of the second half but McCallum was adjudged offside. The Rovers winger was definitely offside in the 80th minute but he was allowed to go on before passing the ball to TOWNLEY to fire the visitors in front. The referee appeared to blow for offside but then changed his mind and allowed the goal to stand. The decision infuriated the Burnley fans, who gave vent to their feelings and, on the final whistle, spilled on to the field to threaten the referee. The official, Mr Horne, who was the Rovers 'keeper's brother, needed a police escort and sought safety in the Main Stand until the angry mob had been dispersed!

Burnley

A. Kaye; W. Bury; A. Lang; W. McFettridge; E. White; J. Keenan; R. Haresnape; W. McColl; C. Lambie; J. Hill; A. Stewart

Blackburn Rovers

J. Horne; T. Brandon; J. Forbes; G. Dewar; W. Almond; J. Forrest; N. McCallum; H. Campbell; Jack Southworth; N. Walton; W. Townley

Attendance: 7,000

11

Match 5
18 October 1890
Burnley 1 Blackburn Rovers 6

Though Rovers lost the toss and therefore had to play up the hill and against the wind, they took the lead after five minutes when WALTON, looking suspiciously offside, took Lofthouse's pass in his stride and fired past the advancing Kaye. Despite some intense Burnley pressure, it was Blackburn who scored the game's next goal in the 16th minute when LOFTHOUSE made a fine run down the right-wing before cutting inside Walker and shooting past Kaye with his left-foot.

Burnley deservedly pulled a goal back in the minutes leading up to half-time. Pennington failed to hold Haresnape's powerful shot and McLARDIE following up put the Clarets back in the game.

Rovers inside-forward Campbell was stretchered off just on half-time but he never appeared for the second half.

Though playing with ten men, the visitors were the far superior team in the second half and extended their lead in the opening minutes of the second period when WALTON scored from close range. Rovers went further ahead a few minutes later as SOUTHWORTH headed home Hall's pin-point cross. Rovers with the wind now at their backs were in complete control and after Burnley's Hill, who wasn't really fully fit, was forced to retire, scored two more goals through BARTON and SOUTHWORTH.

In the last few minutes of the game, the visitors could have added to their score but Kaye in the Burnley goal produced a couple of fine saves.

Burnley
A. Kaye; J. Walker; A. Lang; W. McFettridge; D. Spiers; J. Keenan; R. Haresnape; J. Oswald; A. McLardie; A. Stewart; J. Hill

Blackburn Rovers
R. Pennington; T. Brandon; J. Forbes; J. Barton; G. Dewar; J. Forrest; J. Lofthouse; H. Campbell; Jack Southworth; N. Walton; C. Hall

Attendance: 10,000

Match 6
22 November 1890
Blackburn Rovers 5 Burnley 2

Heavy rain fell throughout this East Lancashire derby, a match Blackburn Rovers began in positive fashion, forcing Kaye in the Burnley goal to make three or four good saves in the opening minutes.

Burnley almost took the lead with their first attack of the game, McLardie being pulled back as he was about to shoot with only Gow to beat. From the resulting free-kick, Lambie's effort was deflected behind for a corner from which the Clarets opened the scoring. Oswald's accurate corner-kick found PLACE and he beat Gow from the edge of the area with the game just nine minutes old. Burnley went further ahead after twenty minutes when following good work by Lambie and Marr, McLARDIE fired high into the roof of the net to round off a good move by the visitors. Oswald had the ball in the Rovers' net as the home side came under increasing pressure but the referee disallowed it for offside. The Rovers' goal had a number of narrow escapes towards the end of the first half but ten minutes into the second period, TOWNLEY pulled a goal back after good work down the left-wing by Forrest and Walton, meeting Lofthouse's pin-point cross with a firm header that gave Kaye little chance. Rovers' equalising goal on the hour mark was an unusual one. WALTON's long range effort seemed to be drifting wide and in fact was left by Burnley 'keeper Kaye only for it to hit a divot and bounce into the net! A minute later and WALTON netted again to give Rovers the lead, converting another fine cross by Lofthouse.

Place missed a chance to level things up before Rovers extended their lead through SOUTHWORTH. With the light fading fast, the home side scored their fifth and final goal in the closing minutes though visibility was so poor, it is not known who the scorer was, though the light can't have been that bad as Burnley fans claimed the ball had been out of play!

Blackburn Rovers

J. Gow; H. Garstang; J. Forbes; J. Barton; G. Dewar; J. Forrest; J. Lofthouse; C. Hall; Jack Southworth; N. Walton; W. Townley

Burnley

A. Kaye; J. Walker; A. Lang; W. McFettridge; D. Spiers; J. Keenan; J. Oswald; A. McLardie; C. Lambie; R. Marr; W. Place snr

Attendance: 4,000

Match 7
26 September 1891
Blackburn Rovers 3 Burnley 3

Burnley's left-winger James Hill arrived at Bank Top Station to see the train by which the team travelled the 12 miles to Blackburn, steam out of the station. By the time he arrived at Ewood Park, ten minutes into the game, the Clarets were 2-0 down.

Rovers' first goal against the ten men of Burnley came after two minutes when Chippendale's cross found SOUTHWORTH unmarked in front of goal and he scored from point-blank range. Blackburn's WALTON scored his side's second goal six minutes later when, following more good work on the right by Chippendale, he crashed his pin-point cross against the inside of the upright and into the net past the startled Hillman.

Following Hill's eventual arrival, the Clarets got back into the game and came close on a number of occasions through Bowes and McLardie. Bowes in fact shaped to shoot into an empty net but the referee pulled him up for a handling offence. LANG pulled a goal back after 35 minutes when his long-range shot caught Horne completely by surprise. Both Horne and Hillman were called into action before the break but at half-time there was no change in the scoreline, Rovers leading 2-1.

Forbes, the Rovers right-back, seemed to punch a Lang shot over the bar but despite all the appeals from the Burnley players, the referee only gave a corner. Play went to the other end and Hillman made a couple of memorable saves as Rovers pressed hard for a third goal. However, Burnley drew level in the 61st minute when NICOL cut inside McKeown and fired home a tremendous left-foot shot that entered Horne's net via the underside of the bar. The Clarets then took the lead when McLARDIE received the ball on the halfway line and completely outpaced the Rovers defence before shooting past the advancing Horne. Hillman, in the Burnley goal, celebrated by performing double somersaults!

There were just two minutes remaining when Jack SOUTHWORTH netted his second and Rovers' third goal following more good work by Chippendale who was making his debut for the home side.

Blackburn Rovers
W. Horne; J. Forbes; T. McKeown, W. Almond; G. Dewar; J. Forrest; H. Chippendale; C. Hall; Jack Southworth; N. Walton; W. Townley

Burnley
J. Hillman; J. Walker; A. Lang; W. McFettridge; D. Spiers; A. Stewart; T. Nicol; A. McLardie; W. Bowes; W. Place snr; J. Hill

Attendance: 4,000

14

Match 8
12 December 1891
Burnley 3 Blackburn Rovers 0

Without doubt, this was one of the most remarkable games ever to take place between the two fierce rivals. The weather was so bad that football was almost impossible. There had been a constant fall of heavy snow for the two hours prior to the kick-off but the referee decided that the game should go ahead.

Burnley took the lead after seven minutes when James Matthew's cross was forced over the line by Tom NICOL. Fifteen minutes later, the Clarets extended their lead when GALBRAITH scored from close range after Arthur had been unable to hold Nicol's powerful shot. There were just ten minutes of the first half remaining when Billy BOWES shot led to the game's first controversial moment. Herbie Arthur the Rovers 'keeper appeared to pick the ball from under the net from the outside and placed the ball for a goal-kick but the referee who was perfectly positioned had no hesitation in awarding the goal!

Trailing 3-0 at half-time, it seemed that Rovers were not going to appear for the second half. Eventually they lined-up with only seven players but matters were made worse a few minutes later when Joe Lofthouse fouled Burnley skipper Alex Stewart and after the two had a brief fight, they were both sent off! This action by the referee caused the remaining Rovers players, with the exception of goalkeeper Herbie Arthur, to walk off!

The referee, J. C. Clegg of Sheffield, waited a few moments for the Rovers side to re-appear and then threw the ball in the air. The Burnley side rushed at goal and though Nicol put the ball between the posts, Arthur's appeal for offside was successful and the game abandoned.

Burnley
J. Hillman; J. Walker; A. Lang; W. McFettridge; J. Matthew; A. Stewart; T. Nicol; W. Bowes; H. Galbraith; A. McLardie; W. Graham

Blackburn Rovers
J. Arthur; J. Forrest; J. Forbes; A. Smith; W. Almond; H. Campbell; J. Lofthouse; C. Hall; Jack Southworth; N. Walton; W. Townley

Attendance: 6,000

Match 9
3 December 1892
Burnley 0 Blackburn Rovers 0

The home side were the first to attack and Claude Lambie, who was playing his first game for the Clarets for almost eighteen months following an horrific injury, went close with a bullet-like header. Rovers forced a succession of corners but nothing came of them. Then, on the half-hour mark, Lambie shot home from an acute angle but the referee disallowed the 'goal' on the grounds that the Burnley centre-forward had handled the ball!

Lambie was having a good game on his return to the Burnley side and just before half-time brought a good save out of Walton. The Clarets right-winger Crabtree took a hefty blow in the ribs from Forbes and had to leave the pitch, taking no further part in the game.

In the closing minutes of this hard fought game, Burnley should have scored when Hill beat a couple of defenders but delayed his shot with only Walton to beat despite the loud cries of 'shoot, shoot'.

That the game remained goalless was in the main due to the fine form of both goalkeepers who coped extremely well with a slippy ball.

Burnley
J. Hillman; T. Nicol; A. Lang; G. King; J. Matthew; W. Bowes; J. Crabtree; T. Chambers; C. Lambie; J. Hill; W. Graham

Blackburn Rovers
N. Walton; J. Murray; J. Forbes; G. Dewar; G. Anderson; H. Marshall; H. Chippendale; H. Campbell; Jack Southworth; C. Hall; J. Bowdler

Attendance: 9,000

Match 10
17 December 1892
Blackburn Rovers 2 Burnley 0

Rovers won the toss and opted to play with a very strong wind behind them. As might be expected, the home side had all the best of the play in the opening period and both Southworth and Campbell brought fine saves out of Hillman in the Burnley goal. The game had been in progress for half-an-hour when BOWDLER scored Rovers' first goal following a misunderstanding between Nicol and Matthews. The Rovers left-winger fired home a powerful shot from 10 yards out though the Burnley 'keeper did manage to get his finger tips to the ball. Rovers went 2-0 up in the 39th minute when SOUTHWORTH scored from close range after Matthews had delayed his clearance. The same player thought he had netted a second goal a few minutes later but he was adjudged offside.

Burnley almost pulled a goal back in the opening minutes of the second half but Crabtree's shot which looked like it was heading for the bottom corner was deflected wide by his team-mate Walter Place senior.

Campbell had the ball in the Burnley net but this too was disallowed for offside. There were just five minutes left to play when Burnley's Sandy Lang and Rovers' Jack Southworth received their marching orders. Lang was knocked to the ground and whilst down, received a kick and another as he was getting up. He then proceeded to head-butt Southworth who retaliated by throwing a punch!

As the Burnley wagonette was leaving Ewood Park after the match, a considerable crowd had gathered at the entrance to the ground. Though dispersed by the police, a shower of bricks, stones and mud greeted the Clarets players and officials, many of whom were badly injured.

Blackburn Rovers
N. Walton; J. Murray; J. Forrest; G. Dewar; G. Anderson; H. Marshall; H. Chippendale; H. Campbell; Jack Southworth; W. Sawers; J. Bowdler

Burnley
J. Hillman; T. Nicol; A. Lang; G. Kay; J. Matthew; W. Bowes; J. Crabtree; T. Chambers; C. Lambie; J. Hill; W. Place snr

Attendance: 7,000

Match 11
18 November 1893
Blackburn Rovers 3 Burnley 2

In a game played in a continuous blizzard of snow and a gale force wind, both sides played some football of the highest quality. Burnley goal-keeper Jack Hillman was injured and had to be left out of the side. His replacement was the versatile Walter Place senior, appearing between the posts for the first time in a League game. With the wind at their backs, Rovers took the lead through a rather soft goal. WHITEHEAD's half-hit shot completely deceived the hapless Place. CHIPPENDALE added a dubious second on the half-hour mark before HILL pulled a goal back for Burnley with virtually the last kick of the first half.

With the Clarets now having the wind in their favour, they pushed forward from the start of the second half in search of the equaliser. They almost levelled the scores but Buchanan fired wide from a good position. With Rovers penned into their own half, it seemed only a matter of time before Burnley drew level. However, the home side scored the game's next goal when Whitehead evaded a couple of tackles and crossed for TOWNLEY to put Rovers 3-1 up.

Chippendale wasted a good chance to put the game completely out of Burnley's reach but he shot straight at Place who clung on well to the winger's powerfully-struck shot.

In the closing minutes, BOWES pulled a goal back for the visitors but though they pressed hard in what little time was remaining, the Rovers defence held firm to take both points.

Blackburn Rovers
A. Ogilvie; R. MacFarlane; J. Forrest; G. Dewar; G. Anderson; H. Marshall; H. Chippendale; J. Whitehead; Jack Southworth; C. Hall; W. Townley

Burnley
W. Place snr; T. McLintock; A. Lang; G. King; J. Espie; A. Livingstone; A. Brady; R. Buchanan; W. Bowes; P. Turnbull; J. Hill

Attendance: 3,000

Match 12
23 December 1893
Burnley 1 Blackburn Rovers 0

In another game played in windy conditions, Burnley captain Jimmy Hill won the toss and elected to play with the wind behind his team. The Clarets almost took the lead in their first attack but Murray kicked off the line from Townley. Nicol then came close with a powerful shot that was · deflected wide of the target with Ogilvie beaten.

Townley again came close for Rovers but then it was the turn of Burnley. Brady and Turnbull almost opened the scoring but Ogilvie was equal to anything the Clarets forwards could throw at him. After weathering this storm, Rovers ended the half the stronger side, forcing Hillman into a number of impressive saves.

In the second half, Livingstone robbed Chippendale and then beat Whitehead before unleashing a terrific shot that rattled Ogilvie's left-hand post. The ball rebounded to HILL who made no mistake from close-in.

The goal only served to inspire the visitors to push forward and though they left gaps at the back, the Clarets forwards and in particular Espie failed to take advantage.

Rovers were unlucky not to equalise due to a mixture of fine keeping by Jack Hillman and a catalogue of misses from both Townley and Hall.

Burnley

J. Hillman; T. Nicol; T. McLintock; J. Mullineux; J. Crabtree; A. Livingstone; A. Brady; P. Turnbull; J. Espie; W. Bowes; J. Hill

Blackburn Rovers

A. Ogilvie; J. Murray; T. Brandon; J. Forrest; G. Dewar; H. Marshall; H. Chippendale; J. Whitehead; J. Sorley; C. Hall; W. Townley

Attendance: 13,000

Match 13
17 November 1894
Blackburn Rovers 1 Burnley 0

The Clarets had the better of the opening exchanges and could quite easily have taken the lead in the 5th minute when Bowes' shot from the edge of the area took a deflection off Brandon's leg and scraped the top of the bar. When Rovers did attack they found Hillman in fine form but it was Burnley who were the better side in a goalless first half with both Nicol grazing the post and Turnbull sending a powerful shot inches wide of the target. With the wind now behind them, Rovers started the second half in a far more confident mood. Hillman made a couple of good saves before Stuart had to be helped off the field after a collision with Crabtree.

A few minutes later, Hillman, Burnley's burly custodian, made an outstanding save but then in the 63rd minute, he was beaten when a shot from CHIPPENDALE, which everybody thought would be cleared by Crabtree crept between the two of them and into the far corner of the net. Though it was one of the softest goals in the history of the East Lancashire Derbies, it brought the game to life.

Burnley though never recovered from this disaster as Rovers pushed forward in search of a second goal. Both Gordon and Stuart had chances to extend the home side's lead but their shots were well saved by Hillman. The Burnley defence stood firm but the Clarets forwards, especially Turnbull and McKnight, missed what few opportunities did come their way in the second half.

Blackburn Rovers
A. Ogilvie; T. Brandon; J. Murray; J. Forrest; G. Anderson; T. Cleghorn;
J. Haydock; J. Whitehead; J. Stuart; P. Gordon; H. Chippendale
Burnley
J. Hillman; J. Crabtree; T. McLintock; W. Place snr; J. Espie;
A. Livingstone; T. Nicol; J. McKnight; P. Turnbull; W. Bowes; J. Hill
Attendance: 7,000

Match 14
12 January 1895
Burnley 2 Blackburn Rovers 1

With both teams in the leading pack in the First Division, the outcome of this match was of great importance. Prior to this game, the Clarets were three points behind Rovers but with two games in hand.

After a week of heavy frost and snowfalls, the Turf Moor surface was rock hard but a sprinkling of sand ensured that, on the whole, the players kept their feet. One player who didn't was Rovers' Whitehead who slipped with the goal at his mercy. Burnley's Hill and Place went close with powerful shots before the former brought a fine save out of Ogilvie in the Rovers' goal.

The Clarets took the lead in the 31st minute when Place's shot hit the crossbar before rebounding into a ruck of players. BOWES was the first to react, sending in an unstoppable drive into the roof of the Ogilvie's net. Burnley continued to press forward and shots rained in on Ogilvie's goal from all directions and though Rovers occasionally broke away, the first half definitely belonged to the home side, especially after Tom McLINTOCK had made it 2-0 in the closing stages of the first period. The Burnley full-back had sent in a long-range shot from fully 40 yards, which entered the Rovers' net through a crowd of players. It was only during the interval that the scorer was known!

When the players returned to the field after the interval, the wind had developed into a gale and was blowing into Hillman's face. However, Turnbull almost added a third for the Clarets but his shot was held up in the wind, allowing Ogilvie to make a comfortable save. Rovers did reduce the arrears when KILLEEN fired home from close range despite appeals from the Burnley defenders that there had been a handling infringement prior to the 'goal'.

Rovers made desperate efforts to draw level but couldn't find a way through the well-organised Burnley defence.

Burnley
J. Hillman; J. Crabtree; T. McLintock; W. Place snr; J. Espie;
A. Livingstone; T. Nicol; W. Bowes; P. Turnbull; J. Hill; W. Place jnr
Blackburn Rovers
A. Ogilvie; T. Brandon; J. Murray; J. Forrest; G. Anderson; T. Cleghorn;
P. Gordon; J. Whitehead; J. Sorley; E. Killeen; H. Chippendale
Attendance: 10,000

Match 15
5 October 1895
Blackburn Rovers 1 Burnley 0

A heavy downpour just an hour or so prior to kick-off did not deter the
Burnley fans from making the short journey to Ewood Park but they must
have been disappointed with their sides showing.

Livingstone had an early chance for the Clarets but he was fouled as
he shaped to shoot. From the resulting free-kick, Ogilvie saved well and
set up a chance for Hargreaves who connected with the 'keeper's long
punt downfield only to head just over the bar. A long shot from Livingstone appeared to be going wide but Ogilvie, who could quite easily have
left the ball, got a touch that almost deflected the ball into the net.

Shortly afterwards came the only goal of the game as Tatham failed to
hold Whitehead's shot and CHIPPENDALE followed up to push the ball
home past a static Burnley defence. The goal instilled far greater confidence into Rovers and they came close to extending their lead just before
the interval when Killeen's shot scraped the upright.

In the second half, Rovers continued to dominate the game. Attack
after attack was made on the Burnley goal but Tatham was in fine form.
The Clarets' one and only chance of the second half came in the 72nd
minute when Nicol dribbled his way into the Blackburn area before
shooting against the post. The ball was cleared only for it to find its way
back into the area shortly afterwards – Nicol poked the ball past Ogilvie
but was adjudged offside!

Blackburn Rovers
A. Ogilvie; T. Brandon; J. Murray; G. Dewar; G. Anderson; T. Cleghorn;
J. Hargreaves; J. Whitehead; P. Turnbull; E. Killeen; H. Chippendale
Burnley
W. Tatham; J. Reynolds; T. McLintock; J. Taylor; W. Place snr;
A. Livingstone; T. Nicol; W. Bowes; J. Davidson; W. Place jnr;
H. Robertson
Attendance: 3,500

Match 16
13 April 1896
Burnley 6 Blackburn Rovers 0

This Easter Monday fixture kicked off at 5.30 pm, the Clarets kicking down the slope with the wind at their backs.

Walter PLACE senior scored Burnley's opening goal after 10 minutes and though the home side had many opportunities to extend their lead, it wasn't until midway through the first half that they did so. Porter let in McEleny and he crossed for NICOL who made no mistake from close-in. Within minutes, Robertson had brought a fine save out of Ogilvie, who tipped the centre-forward's goal-bound shot over the bar.

Rovers had a brief spell of pressure during which Tatham had a couple of shots to save but it was Burnley who went further ahead when NICOL shot home following good work by McEleny and Roberston. Just before half-time, Burnley thought they had scored again when Hill's shot appeared to have crossed the line before Ogilvie scooped it clear.

Though the visitors had the wind behind them in the second-half, they were completely outplayed by the Clarets. ROBERTSON added a fourth for the home side when Ogilvie failed to hold his shot and he followed up to place the ball into the unguarded net. Four minutes later, Place sent in a beautiful cross that NICOL volleyed into the roof of the net off the underside of the bar for his hat-trick.

With Tatham a virtual spectator, the Clarets pushed forward in search of a sixth goal and they were rewarded five minutes from time when ROBERTSON met Nicol's cross to head home. In the few minutes that remained, Burnley could have added to their score but Ogilvie made good saves from Robertson and Hill.

Burnley
W. Tatham; J. Reynolds; T. McLintock; W. Place snr; C. McEleny; J. Taylor; T. Nicol; J. Hill; H. Robertson; J. Davidson; W. Place jnr

Blackburn Rovers
A. Ogilvie; T. Brandon; W. Porter; G. Hannah; J. Yarwood; G. Dewar; J. Whitehead; J. Parkinson; J. Hargreaves; G. Whalley; H. Chippendale

Attendance: 5,000

Match 17
3 October 1896
Blackburn Rovers 3 Burnley 2

There was a sensational start to this East Lancashire Derby as the visitors took the lead after only twenty seconds. Straight from the kick-off, Robertson hit the ball out to the left where Place made good ground before crossing for BOWES to shoot past Joy in the Rovers goal.

Rovers defence seemed completely disorganised and were lucky not to go further behind as Joy made a good save from Roberston and Brandon kicked Hill's goal-bound header off the line. Burnley were awarded a penalty after Killeen had tripped Hill and though Joy got his fingertips to McCluggage's spot-kick, he couldn't prevent the ball from crossing the line. However, Brandon had encroached into the penalty area and the referee awarded the kick to be retaken. This time McCLUGGAGE, the Burnley skipper made no mistake, sending the Rovers 'keeper the wrong way. There were no further goals before the interval for, though the Clarets forwards were dangerous, they found the Rovers defence in a more determined mood.

Just when it seemed likely that Burnley would at last succeed in pulling off their first victory in a league match at Ewood Park, Rovers showed a great improvement in their play. Haddow, in the Burnley goal came under a great deal of pressure, finally being beaten by a DEWAR free-kick. Shortly afterwards the referee awarded the home side a penalty after Taylor had fouled Wilmington as he cut inside to shoot. It was a dubious decision as the offence seemed to have taken place outside the area. ANDERSON took the kick, giving Haddow no chance as he levelled the scores.

CHIPPENDALE then fired Rovers in front and though, during the closing minutes, Burnley came close to grabbing a deserved equaliser when Hill sent a shot against Joy's right-hand upright, it just wasn't to be!

Blackburn Rovers

W. Joy; T. Brandon; E. Killeen; G. Dewar; G. Anderson; A. Houlker; T. Wilmington; H. Chippendale; T. Terney; J. Wilkes; J. Campbell

Burnley

D. Haddow; T. Nicol; T. McLintock; W. Place snr; J. Brae; J. Taylor; T. Warburton; J. Hill; H. Robertson; W. Bowes; W. Place jnr

Attendance: 9,000

Match 18
7 November 1896
Burnley 0 Blackburn Rovers 1

Heavy rain had fallen from early morning and the mist that hung over the ground gave rise to a fear that the game would not be completed.

Defences dominated the first half-hour with neither side being able to find a way through to test the 'keepers. Then in the 32nd minute, Burnley centre-forward Robertson burst through the Rovers defence and crashed a great shot against the underside of Ogilvie's crossbar. The Rovers 'keeper was completely beaten but there was no Clarets forward following up and Dewar cleared the ball to safety.

Burnley had the better of the exchanges in the minutes that remained of the first half and should have had a penalty when Killeen 'handled' Walter Place senior's shot but the referee remarkably turned away their appeals. Ogilvie then produced a breathtaking save from the same player before Rovers broke away and, in the last minute of the first half, scored through CAMPBELL who converted Chippendale's deep cross from the right.

The goal scored against the run of play gave Rovers confidence and they completely dominated the second half. That they didn't add to their lead was due in no small part to the goalkeeping of Tatham. In fact, Rovers scorer Campbell became so infuriated with Tatham's fine form, that he barged the Burnley 'keeper into the upright even though the referee's whistle had already gone for offside – the referee had words with the Blackburn forward when perhaps a sending-off would have been more appropriate!

Burnley
W. Tatham; J. Reynolds; T. McLintock; W. Place snr; T. Nicol; J. Taylor; J. Davidson; J. Hill; H. Robertson; W. Bowes; W. Place jnr

Blackburn Rovers
A. Ogilvie; T. Brandon; G. Anderson; T. Booth; G. Dewar; E. Killeen; H. Chippendale; J. Whitehead; J. Hargreaves; J. Wilkes; J. Campbell

Attendance: 5,000

Match 19
21 April 1898
Blackburn Rovers 1 Burnley 3

In 1897-98, Burnley were the Second Division Champions and Rovers finished one off the bottom of the First Division. In those days it was customary for the bottom two clubs in the top flight and the top sides from the Second Division to play 'Test Matches' to decide which two should be numbered among the sixteen clubs of the First Division. There was no automatic promotion and relegation as we know it today.

The only noteworthy event of a fairly tame first half came in the 33rd minute when Rovers were awarded an indirect free-kick some 30 yards out. Booth's effort looked like going into the net untouched, Hillman making sure it would go harmlessly past him but as the ball landed, BRIERCLIFFE appeared from nowhere to head the ball into the net! This misunderstanding gave Rovers the lead and they crossed over a goal in front.

The second half was only five minutes old when Morrison's centre was dropped by Carter and TOMAN tapped the ball into the empty net. Rovers almost took the lead a minute later as Hargreaves powerful shot brought a magnificent save out of Hillman. However, Burnley went ahead in the 61st minute with a carbon copy of their opening goal. Morrison made a darting run down the right and crossed for TOMAN to force home his and the Clarets' second goal. Five minutes later, the Burnley centre-forward completed his hat-trick – Morrison kept the ball in play with his head whilst lying on the ground and, as Beveridge crossed into the area, TOMAN arrived unmarked to shoot past Carter.

In the dying minutes, the home side thought they had pulled a goal back but Wilkes' shot was brilliantly saved by the Clarets England international 'keeper Jack Hillman.

With almost the last kick of the game, Morrison burst through for Burnley and though his shot appeared to go behind, it ended up in the back of Carter's goal, having broken the side netting!

Blackburn Rovers
J. Carter; T. Brandon; E. Killeen; T. Booth; G. Anderson; H. Marshall; T. Briercliffe; B. Hulse; J. Hargreaves; J. Wilkes; J. Campbell

Burnley
J. Hillman; J. Reynolds; T. McLintock; D. Beveridge; J. Taylor; A. Livingstone; T. Morrison; J. Ross; W. Toman; W. Bowes; W. Place jnr

Attendance: 8,000

25

Match 20
23 April 1898
Burnley 2 Blackburn Rovers 0

The second Test Match at Turf Moor was a fairly dour affair, especially in the first half which provided little in the way of excitement. Hillman, in the Burnley goal, only touched the ball once in the opening 45 minutes and that was from a long-range shot by Proudfoot. Carter was in fine form but he, too, only had a couple of shots to save in the first period.

When the second half got underway, the Clarets were soon reduced to ten men as Morrison sustained a hand injury that forced him out of the action. This didn't deter the home side and after Toman had brought a fine save out of Carter, the same player smashed a close-range shot against the crossbar.

Burnley took the lead in the 53rd minute when following good work by Morrison and Toman, ROSS fired home from fully 30 yards, his shot completely deceiving Carter in the Rovers goal.

The ten men of Burnley continued to make all the running and Toman came close following good work by Place. TOMAN the Clarets centre-forward eventually scored his side's second goal in the 80th minute when Carter's goal-kick landed straight at his feet and he shot into an empty net!

Proudfoot did have a good chance to reduce the arrears a minute later but Hillman was equal to the Rovers centre-forward's effort. The final action of the match saw Place shoot wide from in front of an open goal – had the ball gone between the posts, which it should have done, then Burnley's victory margin would have been truly reflective!

Burnley
J. Hillman; J. Reynolds; T. McLintock; D. Beveridge; J. Taylor; A. Livingstone; T. Morrison; J. Ross; W. Toman; W. Bowes; W. Place jnr

Blackburn Rovers
J. Carter; J. Glover; E. Killeen; H. Marshall; G. Anderson; A. Houlker; F. Moreland; J. Hargreaves; J. Proudfoot; J. Wilkes; J. Campbell

Attendance: 12,000

26

Match 21
26 November 1898
Burnley 2 Blackburn Rovers 0

The game had only been in progress little more than five minutes when Rovers inside-forward Moreland, back helping his defence, handled in the area and the referee awarded a penalty. McLINTOCK sent Carter the wrong way to give the home side an early lead. The rest of the first half was a fairly dull affair with few chances being created by either side and at the interval, the score remained 1-0 in Burnley's favour.

The second half proved far more exciting with both sides going all out on attack. Rovers should have equalised when Williams was put through but with only Hillman to beat, he screwed his shot wide.

The Clarets went further ahead with just ten minutes remaining when TOMAN managed to evade a couple of challenges before shooting past the advancing Carter. The latter stages of the game saw Rovers having to defend in depth as Burnley pressed forward in search of a third goal. Carter was called upon to make two or three more saves; on one occasion he was extremely lucky, the ball hitting him as he lay on the ground!

Burnley
J. Hillman; W. Place snr; T. McLintock; F. Barron; J. Taylor; A. Livingstone; T. Morrison; J. Ross; W. Toman; W. Bowes; W. Place jnr

Blackburn Rovers
J. Carter; T. Brandon; R. Crompton; T. Booth; R. Haworth; P. Chambers; W. Williams; B. Hulse; J. Jackson; F. Moreland; D. Hurst

Attendance: 12,000

Match 22
26 December 1898
Blackburn Rovers 0 Burnley 2

Daylight robbery was the name of the game as Burnley came away from the Boxing Day fixture at Ewood Park with both points. Rovers did most of the attacking and as early as the fourth minute had the ball in the net but Jackson's effort was disallowed for offside. Hillman in the Burnley goal made good saves from long-range efforts by Hulse and Briercliffe and then the woodwork came to his rescue when Blackburn's header from Garstang's cross rattled the crossbar.

The home side continued to do all the pressing and Jackson brought a fine save out of the Burnley 'keeper but, three minutes before half-time, the Clarets took the lead completely against the run of play when a long hopeful punt upfield was well controlled by TOMAN who ran on to shoot past the advancing Carter to put Burnley 1-0 up.

Rovers started the second half in similar fashion to the first with Jackson and then Hulse having golden opportunities to equalise. As the game wore on it appeared to be only a matter of time before Rovers drew level as the Burnley goal had a charmed life. Hillman made saves that on occasions he knew little about and both full-backs, Reynolds and McLintock cleared off the goal-line. However, midway through the second half in another rare Burnley breakaway, ROSS scored the Clarets' second goal when his long-range shot took a deflection off a Rovers defender to completely wrong-foot Carter in the Blackburn goal.

Rovers continued to attack and the Burnley goal had some miraculous escapes but, despite having most of the possession and attacking for virtually the whole of the ninety minutes, they couldn't turn their superiority into goals.

Blackburn Rovers
J. Carter; T. Brandon; R. Crompton; T. Booth; G. Anderson; P. Chambers; J. Garstang; B. Hulse; J. Jackson; F. Blackburn; T. Briercliffe

Burnley
J. Hillman; J. Reynolds; T. McLintock; F. Barron; W. Place snr; A. Livingstone; T. Morrison; J. Ross; W. Toman; W. Bowes; W. Place jnr

Attendance: 20,000

Match 23
7 October 1899
Burnley 1 Blackburn Rovers 0

Playing with the slope and wind in their favour, Rovers made all the early running and both Hulse and Hurst brought fine saves out of Burnley 'keeper Hillman, When play switched to the other end, the Clarets centre-forward Taylor rattled the visitors' crossbar before the ball entered the net but his effort was disallowed for offside. Burnley continued to attack and Chadwick hit the upright when it seemed easier to score! Barron also wasted a good chance for the Clarets, lifting the ball over the bar from close in with only Knowles to beat.

It was only towards the end of the first half that Rovers came back into the game with Anderson bringing a fine save out of Hillman.

Morrison went close for Burnley in the opening exchanges of the second half and Chadwick's header just cleared the bar with Knowles a spectator. Taylor's first time shot was headed from under his own crossbar by Brandon and then Place grazed the outside of the post with a blistering drive.

Burnley eventually scored the goal that their all-round play had deserved. For following Morrison's corner, BOWES scrambled the ball over the line with Rovers defenders appealing for handball. Taylor came close to adding a second for the home side but his well-placed shot from the edge of the area was turned round the post by Knowles. Chadwick's header seemed over the line when the Rovers 'keeper clawed it back into play but the referee waved away Burnley's claim for a goal.

The Clarets attacked incessantly and Chadwick was desperately unlucky on two or three occasions before Place had the misfortune to shoot against the inside of Knowles' left-hand upright. There is no doubt that Burnley deserved to win but with a little more luck, the margin could have been much greater!

Burnley
J. Hillman; T. Woolfall; T. McLintock; F. Barron; W. Bannister;
A. Livingstone; T. Morrison; W. Bowes; J. Taylor; E. Chadwick;
W. Place snr

Blackburn Rovers
A. Knowles; T. Brandon; R. Crompton; R. Haworth; T. Booth; A. Houlker;
G. Anderson; J. Crook; B. Hulse; F. Blackburn; D. Hurst

Attendance: 12,855

Match 24
1 January 1900
Blackburn Rovers 2 Burnley 0

Seldom can the Clarets have given a worse display than in this New Year's Day encounter at Ewood Park. Early on in the game, Place had a good opportunity to open the scoring for the visitors but he blasted his shot high over the Rovers' bar. Shortly afterwards, Burnley's outside-right Hannigan failed to make the most of good work by Morrison and Chadwick when he completely missed his kick with only Rovers 'keeper Knowles to beat. Midway through the first half, Rovers lost outside-left Hurst who was forced to retire following a collision with his team-mate Dewhurst! It was soon after Hurst's departure that ten men

Rovers took the lead when DEWHURST latched on to a good through ball by McClure to shoot past Hillman.

Shortly after the resumption, BRIERCLIFFE extended the home side's lead, following up Booth's powerful header, which Hillman was unable to hold. The rest of the second half belonged to Rovers who, despite being one player down, were easily the stronger side. That the Clarets didn't lose by a far greater margin was down to the fact that 'keeper Jack Hillman made some breathtaking saves, one in the final minute from Hulse being out of this world!

Blackburn Rovers
A. Knowles; T. Brandon; R. Crompton; S. McClure; T. Booth; R. Haworth; J. Law; T. Briercliffe; B. Hulse; J. Dewhurst; D. Hurst

Burnley
J. Hillman; T. Woolfall; T. McLintock; F. Barron; J. Taylor; A. Livingstone; R. Hannigan; T. Morrison; E. Chadwick; W. Place snr; J. Miller

Attendance: 14,000

Match 25
8 March 1913
Blackburn Rovers 0 Burnley 1

Both teams were at full strength for this fourth round FA Cup tie, though five of the Rovers side had been on either the injured or sick list in the days leading up to the match. Rovers were certainly the more dangerous in the opening quarter of the game when Jerry Dawson in the Burnley goal was called upon to make good saves from Bradshaw, Aitkenhead and Latheron, the latter after a fine centre by Anthony. Burnley gradually got into the game and Husband shot narrowly over the bar after neat work by Lindley. The Clarets skipper, Tommy Boyle, also came close with a powerful long-range shot, just outside Robinson's right-hand post. Hodgson could, and should, have done better with a free shot on goal on the half-hour mark but shot tamely into the hands of Robinson. Three minutes later, the visitors took the lead when BOYLE headed home Mosscrop's corner. The goal seemed to spur Rovers on and Aitkenhead's shot was headed off the line by Bamford with Dawson well beaten.

The Burnley 'keeper was called into action in the closing stages of the first half, saving at the near post from Danny Shea. Though the Clarets had the better of the first half, Rovers were on top for much of the game after the interval. Dawson made a number of good saves, whilst Boyle

30

and Taylor were prominent at the heart of the Burnley defence, as Blackburn tried to get on level terms. In fact, Burnley could have extended their lead in the closing minutes but as the ball arrived at Lindley's feet, he was taken by surprise and allowed Robinson to take it off his toes!

The receipts for the day, £3,003, were the second highest for any Cup-tie outside the semi-final or final!

Blackburn Rovers
A. Robinson; R. Crompton; A. Cowell; A. Walmsley; P. Smith; W. Bradshaw; J. Simpson; D. Shea; W. Aitkenhead; E. Atheron; W. Anthony

Burnley
J. Dawson; T. Bamford; D. Taylor; W. McLaren; T. Boyle; N. Watson; E. Mosscrop; R. Lindley; B. Freeman; E. Hodgson; W. Husband

Attendance: 42,778

Match 26
8 September 1913
Burnley 1 Blackburn Rovers 2

Rovers attacked straight from the kick-off and Chapman brought Dawson to his knees with a powerful long-range shot. Shea, too, forced the Burnley 'keeper to save by his near post as the visitors continued to press forward. However, it was Burnley who took the lead in the 14th minute when Nesbitt was sent clear, he centred for Hodgson who teed the ball up for FREEMAN and he had the ball in the net before the Rovers defence could react.

The Clarets grew in confidence and Husband shot wide from a good position before Hodgson forced Robinson into saving from his bullet-like header. Rovers equalised in the 33rd minute when, following Hodkinson's corner, SMITH shot home from close range. Shortly afterwards, Taylor the Burnley left-back was forced to leave the field after being injured in a goalmouth melee, leaving the Clarets to play the last ten minutes of the first half with ten men. Even so, it was they who came closest to scoring the next goal when in the final minute of the first half, Lindley's deflected shot rolled along the crossbar before going out for a corner.

The second half was only four minutes old when Rovers took the lead. Following a foul on Latheron, the visitors were awarded a free-kick that

31

was floated into the Burnley penalty area where it was met by CHAP-MAN whose well-struck volley gave Dawson no chance.

Play then became scrappy, though Freeman was impeded as he ran through the Rovers defence. Though goalscoring opportunities were few and far between, Latheron should have extended Rovers' lead in the dying minutes when he missed the easiest chance of the match.

Burnley
J. Dawson; T. Bamford; D. Taylor; G. Halley; T. Boyle; W. Watson; W. Nesbitt; R. Lindley; B. Freeman; E. Hodgson; W. Husband

Blackburn Rovers
A. Robinson; R. Crompton; A. Cowell; A. Walmsley; P. Smith; W. Bradshaw; J. Simpson D. Shea; G. Chapman; E. Latheron; J. Hodkinson

Attendance: 36,000

Match 27
1 January 1914
Blackburn Rovers 0 Burnley 0

The game was only six minutes old when Lindley shot wide of an open goal. The visitors continued to dominate the opening half-an-hour but the former Everton striker Bert Freeman missed three easy chances. First Hodgson put him clean through but he delayed his shot allowing Rovers 'keeper Robinson to take the ball off his toes. Halley then took a free-kick but as he received the ball completely unmarked, the usually prolific Freeman screwed his shot wide. The Burnley centre-forward's third chance came when the entire Rovers defence missed Mosscrop's deeply-hit corner but instead of directing the ball inside the far post, Freeman proceeded to miss the target completely!

Rovers came back into the game for a short spell but on the stroke of half-time, the Clarets can consider themselves unlucky not to have been awarded a penalty as Percy Smith the Blackburn centre-half clearly diverted the ball from the path of Lindley with his hand!

In the second half, Burnley again did most of the attacking and the Rovers' goal led a charmed life whilst Jerry Dawson at the other end was a virtual spectator. Both Lindley and Hodgson wasted good opportunities for opening the scoring for Burnley, the latter lifting the ball over the bar with Robinson out of his goal.

32

Though the game remained goalless, there is no doubt that Burnley ought to have returned to Turf Moor with more than one point.

Blackburn Rovers
A. Robinson; G. Chapman; A. Cowell; A. Walmsley; P. Smith; W. Bradshaw; J. Simpson; D. Shea; W. Aitkenhead; E. Latheron; J. Hodkinson

Burnley
J. Dawson; T. Bamford; D. Taylor; G. Halley; T. Boyle; W. Watson; W. Nesbitt; R. Lindley; B. Freeman; E. Hodgson; E. Mosscrop

Attendance: 48,000

Match 28
28 November 1914
Blackburn Rovers 6 Burnley 0

Present in the 21,673 crowd were a number of wounded British and Belgian soldiers and they witnessed the FA Cup holders' heaviest defeat in a game played at Ewood Park.

Yet it was the Clarets who played the more adventurous football in the opening stages of the game, with Robinson having to make a number of saves, especially from the dangerous Hodgson who was the liveliest of the Burnley forwards.

Rovers took the lead in the 14th minute when DAWSON cut in from the left-wing and fired past his namesake in the Burnley goal. Seven minutes later DAWSON scored his and the home side's second goal following a goalmouth scramble. Sadly, this resulted in Burnley's Tommy Boyle sustaining a nasty leg injury, which resulted in him being stretchered-off. When he returned he went on to the wing and this allowed Rovers' goalscorer DAWSON much more space, which he immediately capitalised on by netting his hat-trick in the 36th minute. Shortly afterwards, Burnley almost pulled a goal back when Mosscrop's centre was turned against the crossbar by Robinson. As it was, Rovers went straight down to the other end where DAWSON headed home Hodkinson's pin-point cross to make the half-time score 4-0 in Rovers' favour with all the goals being scored by Percy Dawson.

Boyle suffered another blow to his injured leg and again had to leave the field for treatment. The ten-men Clarets fell further behind in the 51st minute when TAYLOR had the misfortune to divert Latheron's shot past his own 'keeper for Rovers' fifth goal. Burnley responded by throwing caution to the wind and Walmsley thumped a header against Robinson's crossbar before Crompton cleared off the line with the Rovers 'keeper beaten.

With eight minutes to go, LATHERON registered the game's last goal, to complete the Clarets' misery!

Blackburn Rovers
A. Robinson; R. Crompton; A. Cowell; A. Walmsley; P. Smith; W. Aitkenhead; J. Simpson; D. Shea; P. Dawson; E. Latheron; J. Hodkinson

Burnley
J. Dawson; T. Bamford; D. Taylor; G. Halley; T. Boyle; W. Watson; R. Kelly; R. Lindley; B. Freeman; E. Hodgson; E. Mosscrop

Attendance: 21,673

Match 29
3 April 1915
Burnley 3 Blackburn Rovers 2

Though Rovers had the better of the opening exchanges with both Latheron and Dawson going close, Burnley gradually got on top as the game unfolded.

The Clarets took the lead in the 23rd minute when Mosscrop worked his way to the by-line before pulling the ball back for FREEMAN to head home his first goal at Turf Moor for four months! Both Freeman and Hodgson tested Edge with powerful long-range shots before the Blackburn goal had one particularly narrow escape. Freeman sent in another well-struck shot, which Edge turned against the upright. As the ball lay on the goal-line, Crompton raced back and hacked the ball clear. The slippery conditions were producing a number of errors on both sides but the only other goalmouth incident of note in the first half came when Mosscrop's shot-cum-cross completely fooled Edge and landed in the roof of the net.

Rovers began the second half as they had the first but this time their pressure resulted in a goal as LATHERON took Orr's inch-perfect pass in his stride before shooting past Dawson. Within a minute, Burnley had regained the lead as HODGSON fired home through a crowd of players following excellent approach play by Thorpe and Boyle. Both sides created a number of openings and both Dawson and Edge were called into action but the next goal came from the boot of Burnley's

34

MOSSCROP whose curling left-foot shot beat Edge's valiant dive. Rovers reduced the arrears five minutes from time when Watson was adjudged to have fouled Simpson in the penalty area and CROMPTON crashed home the resulting spot-kick. Rovers custodian Edge, who was the busier of the two 'keepers was called into action yet again in the closing minutes of the game, turning Mosscrop's shot round the post.

Burnley

J. Dawson; T. Bamford; D. Taylor; L. Thorpe; T. Boyle; W. Watson; W. Nesbitt; R. Kelly; B. Freeman; E. Hodgson; E. Mosscrop;

Blackburn Rovers

A. Edge; R. Crompton; A. Cowell; A. Walmsley; P. Smith; W. Aitkenhead; J. Simpson; J. Orr; P. Dawson; E. Latheron; J. Hodkinson

Attendance: 14,000

Match 30
4 November 1916
Burnley 2 Blackburn Rovers 0

There was a sensational start to the first wartime fixture between the two sides, when Bob KELLY fired the Clarets ahead with less than a minute played. The winger, receiving the ball from Freeman, cut inside Crompton before unleashing a powerful shot that beat McIver at his near post.

Rovers almost went 2-0 down minutes later but Hodgson miskicked with the goal at his mercy. The visitors improved as the first half wore on and in fact, had far more possession than the Clarets but couldn't convert any of the chances they created. Burnley, too, had a chance to extend their lead as the half closed but Kelly's shot cannoned off McIver's shins for a corner. With virtually the last kick of the half, LINDLEY netted from close range after good wing play by Kelly.

Kelly grazed the bar in the opening minute of the second period with McIver well beaten but after that, Rovers made all the running. Aitkenhead hit the bar with Dawson out of position and both McGhie and Bradshaw shaved the woodwork with the Burnley 'keeper unsighted. The visitors continued to press forward but couldn't breakdown the resolute Burnley defence.

35

Burnley
J. Dawson; J. Wareing; D. Taylor; J. Yates; T. Boyle; J. Wilde; R. Kelly;
R. Lindley; B. Freeman; E. Hodgson; W. Kellock;

Blackburn Rovers
W. McIver; R. Crompton; A. Pickup; A. Walmsley; P. Smith; W. Bradshaw;
A. McGhie; W. Aitkenhead; G. Chapman; E. Latheron; J. Hodkinson

Attendance: 10,000

Match 31
1 January 1917
Blackburn Rovers 1 Burnley 4

Both sides were handicapped owing to the inability of the soldier members having to play in a military charity match at Preston. With the light drawing in, it was decided to play only 35 minutes each way.

Rovers took the lead on the half-hour mark when James Wilde pushed Hewitt over on the edge of the box and from the resultant free-kick, BRADSHAW curled his shot past the outstretched arms of Jerry Dawson and into the roof of the net. Just before half-time, Cunliffe in the Rovers goal was called into action, saving well from both Lindley and Barber.

Neither team left the field at half-time, changing straight round. Burnley drew level five minutes into the second half when Kehoe crossed to HASTIE whose header proved too strong for Cunliffe, who got his hands to the ball but couldn't prevent it from entering the net. The Clarets centre-forward nearly added a second but his shot clipped the crossbar with Cunliffe beaten. It was now all Burnley and Joe WILDE gave them the lead following a goalmouth scramble. WILDE, the Burnley centre-half, netted his second goal a minute later when Cunliffe dropped a Wadsworth corner and the big pivot smashed the ball home from only a yard out.

Shortly afterwards, LINDLEY's shot was tipped against the post by Cunliffe before nestling in the back of the net. Burnley's last three goals had come in the space of five minutes, giving the visitors a thoroughly deserved victory.

Blackburn Rovers
G. Cunliffe; R. Crompton; A. Cowell; F. Duckworth; I. Maggs; W. Bradshaw;
A. Byrom; T. Byrom; K. Hewitt; W. Richmond; S. Wadsworth

Burnley
J. Dawson; J. Hendrey; Jas Wilde; W. Nesbitt; Jos Wilde; W. Broom;
J. Yates; W. Barber; H. Hastie; R. Lindley; J. Kehoe

Attendance: 3,000

36

Match 32
31 March 1917
Blackburn Rovers 4 Burnley 0

Both sides were well below strength for this game and Burnley who had Blackpool's Cocker 'guesting' for them, also had to borrow two Blackburn juniors – Duckworth and Birch.

The only goal of a rather disappointing first half fell to Blackburn's ORR who having already forced Jerry Dawson into making a save at the foot of his right-hand post, beat the Burnley 'keeper with a downward header in the 35th minute.

Freeman, who had played centre-half in the first half, moved up front in the second half in an attempt to add a little more power to the Burnley forward line. He immediately had a 25-yard shot well saved by Spencer but after that, little was seen of him.

Rovers extended their lead when following three corners taken in quick succession, SMITH netted from close range. The home side were much too strong for the Clarets and BYROM made it 3-0 on the hour mark with a well-placed shot from the edge of the penalty area. RALPH completed the scoring in the latter stages of the game after Dawson had saved well from both Byrom and Green.

Blackburn Rovers
J. Spencer; R. Walmsley; A. Cowell; W. Duckworth; P. Smith; W. Dawson; A. Byrom; J. Orr; O. Ralph; R. Green; J. Duckworth

Burnley
J. Dawson; A. Newton; G. Duckworth; W. Nesbitt; B. Freeman; T. Heslop; J. Birch; H. Hastie; A. Hancock; G. Johnson; R. Cocker

Attendance: 2,000

Match 33
14 April 1917
Burnley 4 Blackburn Rovers 1

Though Burnley appeared in their usual colours of claret and blue, Rovers, who fielded a team that was primarily under military age, wore red.

In a goalless first half, the Clarets had much the better of the play but failed to take any of the chances that came their way. The best of these

37

fell to Bert Freeman who having been put clean through by Hibbert, shot straight at Spencer.

Burnley continued to press forward after the interval but it was Rovers who took the lead completely against the run of play when Hastie missed his kick and let in RALPH who shot past the advancing Dawson.

The home side equalised in the 62nd minute when FREEMAN atoned for his earlier miss with a glorious shot from just outside the penalty area that gave Spencer in the Blackburn goal no chance whatsoever. Freeman then brought a fine save out of the Rovers' keeper but he couldn't hold on to the ball and WOODWARD following up gave the home side the lead. Joe WILDE put the Clarets further ahead a minute later and WOOD-WARD netted his second and Burnley's fourth goal after Spencer had failed to gather Freeman's header cleanly.

Burnley
J. Dawson; Jas Wilde; H. Hastie; R. Lindley; Jos Wilde; G. Johnson; J. Birch; F. Woodward; B. Freeman; W. Hibbert; T. Heslop

Blackburn Rovers
J. Spencer; F. Duckworth; A. Pickup; W. Duckworth; P. Smith; W. Entwistle; J. Atherton; A. Byrom; O. Ralph; R. Green; J. Duckworth

Attendance: 1,000

Match 34
29 September 1917
Blackburn Rovers 3 Burnley 1

Rovers' keeper Gaskell was called upon to make a number of fine saves in the opening quarter-of-an-hour as Ewart and Mitten got the better of the Blackburn defence. Burnley's pressure eventually told when KEHOE shot the visitors ahead midway through the first half. The Clarets almost went 2-0 up a few minutes later but Gaskell again came to the rescue, kicking the ball off Woods' toes as he lay prostrate on the ground. Rovers drew level in the 35th minute when Ralph was upended as he broke through the Burnley defence and BRADSHAW made no mistake from the resulting penalty. Virtually on the stroke of half-time, Rovers were awarded a free-kick which Chapman took quickly to release Bradshaw. The Rovers winger crossed to the far post where RALPH headed the home side in front.

Both goalkeepers were called in to action in the early stages of the second half. There seemed to be no way that either 'keeper would be beaten but on the hour mark, Johnson the Burnley right-back handled Moorcroft's shot and BRADSHAW again netted from the spot. In fact, five minutes from time, Ralph was sent sprawling in the area and the referee had no hesitation in awarding Rovers their third penalty of the match. With a chance of recording a hat-trick of penalties, Bradshaw shot hard and low to Wilcox's left but the Burnley 'keeper made a fine save.

Blackburn Rovers
A. Gaskell; T. Atherton; J. Brindle; J. Boothman; G. Chapman; T. Jacques; R. McArthur; D. Moorcroft; O. Ralph; J. Lucas; W. Bradshaw

Burnley
J. Wilcox; G. Johnson; H. Hastie; R. Lindley; M. Duxbury; T. Heslop; E. Woods; T. Ewart; J. Mitten; G. Duckworth; J. Kehoe;

Attendance: 700

Match 35
6 October 1917
Burnley 6 Blackburn Rovers 1

Burnley centre-forward Bert FREEMAN had already headed against the post when he opened the scoring for the Clarets in the sixth minute. HESLOP added a second for the home side midway through the first half, volleying home Johnson's cross. Burnley's two goalscorers combined for the Clarets' third goal in the 35th minute when wing-half Heslop's pin-point cross picked out FREEMAN whose header sailed over Gaskell in the Rovers goal and entered the net via the underside of the crossbar. In the remaining minutes of the first half, Burnley had further chances to extend their lead but Gaskell made a couple of fine saves.

After the interval, Rovers made their first serious threat on the Burnley goal but Lucas' header was well saved by Quinn. Rovers did reduce the arrears in the 73rd minute when MART headed past Quinn from Duckworth's accurate cross.

Four minutes later, Burnley regained their three-goal lead when WOODS fired home from an acute angle after the Rovers 'keeper had made a fine save from his first effort. FREEMAN then scored the goal of the game, beating three Blackburn defenders in a powerful run from the halfway line before shooting past Gaskell. WOODWARD netted a sixth goal for the Clarets, who but for a ten-minute spell at the beginning of the second half, dominated the game.

Burnley

J. Quinn; W. Nesbitt; H. Hastie; R. Lindley; M. Duxbury; T. Heslop; E. Woods; B. Edwards; B. Freeman; F. Woodward; G. Johnson

Blackburn Rovers

A. Gaskell; T. Atherton; J. Waters; W. Duckworth; J. Boothman; S. Baker; R. McArthur; D. Moorcroft; J. Mart; J. Lucas; F. Forshaw;

Attendance: 1,000

Match 36
13 April 1918
Burnley 3 Blackburn Rovers 0

Blackburn 'keeper Gaskell was called into action on a number of occasions during the opening stages of the match, denying both Adamson and Riley. Burnley were unlucky not to be ahead at half-time but a combination of bad finishing and the woodwork denied the Clarets from taking the lead.

Early in the second half Woods rattled Gaskell's right-hand post and Edwards forced the Rovers 'keeper into making a good save. There were just twenty minutes left when Burnley took the lead through WOODS who cut in from the right and unleashed a powerful left-foot shot that gave Gaskell no chance. Three minutes later, RILEY went close as the Rovers defence appealed for offside and after rounding Gaskell, slotted the ball into the empty net for the home side's second goal. In the 81st minute, EDWARDS scored Burnley's third goal following a mix-up in the Rovers' six-yard box and a minute later Frank Newton brought the save of the match out of Gaskell, but for whom the Clarets would have won by a far greater margin.

Burnley

W. Pollard; W. Finney; W. Newton; A. Newton; R. Lindley; R. Jones; E. Woods; B. Edwards; M. Riley; S. Adamson; F. Newton

Blackburn Rovers

A. Gaskell; J. Birmingham; J. Boothman; W. Duckworth; O. Ralph; J. Waters; E. Calvert; F. Livesey; B. McAdam; J. Ryden; J. Briggs

Attendance: 800

Match 37
20 April 1918
Blackburn Rovers 2 Burnley 1

Rovers took the lead in the second minute of the game when Goodman raced clear of the Burnley defence before pulling the ball back for McADAM to shoot past Pollard. Four minutes later, the Clarets were on level terms when Edwards beat Walmsley and crossed for BRIGGS to force the ball home from close-range. Surprisingly, after these two early goals, chances in the first half were few and far between although Lindley came closest for the visitors when his long-range effort beat Gaskell in the Rovers goal only to strike the foot of the post.

In the second half both sets of forwards missed goalscoring opportunities with Burnley's Frank Newton coming closest with a header which smashed against the bar with Gaskell beaten. With just ten minutes remaining, it appeared that Edwards would score the Clarets' second goal but after rounding Gaskell he underhit his shot, allowing Goodman to get back and clear the danger.

Vaughan thought he had given Rovers the lead but his effort was disallowed for offside. However, McADAM netted the winner for Rovers in the closing minutes with a shot that struck the post before entering the net.

Blackburn Rovers
A. Gaskell; J. Birmingham; R. Walmsley; W. Duckworth; J. Boothman; A. Houlker; F. Livesey; B. McAdam; S. Goodman; M. Vaughan; O. Ralph
Burnley
W. Pollard; W. Finney; W. Newton; A. Newton; R. Lindley; R. Jones; H. Hastie; B. Edwards; J. Briggs; F. Newton; J. Kehoe
Attendance: 1,000

Match 38
5 October 1918
Burnley 0 Blackburn Rovers 1

The home side dominated the early stages of the game, forcing several corners in quick succession. Though Gaskell in the Rovers goal made fine saves from Clarkson and Freeman, he could do very little about Ormerod's rising drive, which smashed against the crossbar. The Clarets inside-forward went close on the half-hour mark, his powerful header going inches wide of Gaskell's right-hand post. Burnley did have the ball in the net just before half-time when Grant's shot was deflected past the

41

stranded Blackburn 'keeper by Waters. The referee adjudged that the ball had already gone out of play prior to it arriving at the feet of Grant.

Burnley continued to dominate the proceedings, restricting Rovers to just a couple of breakaways. However, from one of these, CORNTHWAITE scored the only goal of the game in the 75th minute. Levus made the most of his pace before crossing for the Rovers outside-left to side-foot the ball home from close-range.

The Clarets forwards worked hard but couldn't find a way past the resolute Rovers defence, though they came close in the dying moments of the match when Freeman's shot was deflected by Boothman, only for the ball to land on the top of the crossbar before going out for a corner. The flag kick caused panic in the Rovers six-yard box but, yet again, Burnley couldn't capitalise on the situation.

Burnley
R. Greenwood; M. Ormerod; W. Finney; R. Lindley; T. Emmott; A. Newton; B. Grant; G. Cunningham; B. Freeman; J. Ormerod; J. Clarkson

Blackburn Rovers
A. Gaskell; J. Birmingham; J. Waters; W. Duckworth; J. Boothman; O. Ralph; W. Levus; F. Livesey; D. Cooper; D. Gibson; R. Cornthwaite

Attendance: 1,000

Match 39
12 October 1918
Blackburn Rovers 3 Burnley 4

The opening exchanges were fast and furious with Rovers 'keeper Gaskell being called upon to make a brave save at the feet of the onrushing Lindley. The Clarets wing-half was in fine form throughout the game and it was from one of his probing passes that Bert FREEMAN gave Burnley the lead. It didn't last long for within two minutes, BOOTHMAN had equalised for Rovers, following up to score after his first shot had hit the post.

Burnley did most of the attacking and midway through the first half, FREEMAN headed in Grant's pin-point cross. Rovers came back strongly and Wilcox in the Burnley goal made two excellent saves. Fine work by Levus ended in RUSHTON levelling the scores before FREEMAN completed his hat-trick with the best goal of the game. Picking the ball up on the halfway line, he rounded three Rovers defenders before slotting the ball past the advancing Gaskell. Just before half-time, Finney was adjudged to have fouled Boothman in the area and, from the resulting penalty-kick, LEVUS made sure the sides went in all-square at 3-3.

Early in the second half, CUNNINGHAM restored the Clarets lead following good work by Freeman. There was no further scoring though Rushton had missed an excellent opportunity to level the scores but the Rovers centre-forward sliced his shot inches past Wilcox's right-hand post.

Blackburn Rovers
A. Gaskell; T. Brandon; J. Birmingham; W. Duckworth; J. Boothman; O. Ralph; W. Levus; F. Livesey; H. Rushton; H. Rothwell; R. Haworth

Burnley
J. Wilcox; W. Finney; W. Newton; H. Hastie; R. Lindley; A. Newton; B. Grant; G. Cunningham; B. Freeman; J. Cowgill; J. Clarkson

Attendance: 1,500

Match 40
19 April 1919
Blackburn Rovers 2 Burnley 4

The game was less than five minutes old when Rovers- full-back Duckworth handled just outside the penalty area. Burnley captain Tommy BOYLE drove the ball wide of Robinson's despairing dive to give the visitors an early lead. Only eleven minutes had been played when the Clarets extended their lead. Nesbitt made progress down the right before crossing for KELLY to shoot home from close-range. Burnley remained on top for the rest of the first half but couldn't add to their lead.

The second half was barely a minute old when Danny SHEA reduced the arrears, fastening on to Wilde's well-directed header. Burnley continued to dominate the game and it was no surprise when KELLY scored his second and the Clarets' third goal, following a maze-like run. LINDLEY scored the visitors fourth goal after good work by Freeman and Mosscrop.

With almost the last kick of the game, SHEA scored his and Rovers second goal from the penalty-spot after the former West Ham United forward had been upended in the box.

Blackburn Rovers
A. Robinson; J. Barton; F. Duckworth; A. Walmsley; P. Smith; J. Boothman; A. McGhie; D. Shea; S. Wakeley; P. Holland; J. Kerr

Burnley
J. Dawson; L. Smelt; Jas Wilde; W. Taylor; T. Boyle; W. Watson; W. Nesbitt; R. Kelly; B. Freeman; R. Lindley; E. Mosscrop

Attendance: 4,000

Match 41
26 April 1919
Burnley 5 Blackburn Rovers 1

The final game of the season saw both teams wear black arm bands in respect for the Burnley and Blackburn players who had lost their lives during the hostilities.

NORRIS, who was making his Burnley debut opened the scoring for the home side after just two minutes, taking Kelly's measured pass in his stride and firing past McIvor. The home goal was rarely threatened in the opening stages and it came as no surprise when on a quarter-of-an-hour, the Clarets extended their lead through KELLY. Norris came close on a couple of occasions before Burnley went 3-0. CLARKSON and Norris played a neat one-two before the former fired home from the edge of the area. Rovers' only efforts of note in a disappointing first half came from McGhie and Green.

Boyle, who had gone off injured with torn shoulder ligaments towards the end of the first half, returned for the second period but went to play at outside-right.

The second half was played in an almost continuous hailstorm but this didn't deter the Clarets who scored further goals through KELLY and NESBITT. Freeman, the Clarets' leading scorer, went close with a powerful header whilst the injured Boyle rattled the crossbar with a tremendous long-range shot.

Rovers eventually got on the scoresheet in the dying moments of the game when GREEN's shot from close-range appeared to go into the net off Thorpe.

Burnley
W. Sewell; L. Smelt; T. Bamford; L. Thorpe; T. Boyle; T. Watson; W. Nesbitt; R. Kelly; B. Freeman; P. Norris; J. Clarkson

Blackburn Rovers
W. McIvor; J. McFadyen; J. Boothman; A. Walmsley; P. Smith; T. Heaton; A. McGhie; J. Carter; T. Byrom; P. Holland; R. Green

Attendance: 18,000

Match 42
13 September 1919
Blackburn Rovers 2 Burnley 3

The first Football League game for over four years was full of incidents. Rovers were the first to find the net when following good work on the right by Shea, DAWSON beat his namesake at the near post with a well-placed header. After quarter-of-an-hour, the Clarets were awarded a penalty after Walmsley had handled Taylor's goal-bound shot. Boyle took the spot-kick but his shot was brilliantly turned over the bar by Robinson. The Clarets eventually equalised after 26 minutes when Walmsley deflected Mosscrop's centre into the path of TAYLOR whose shot from point-blank range gave Robinson no chance.

Dawson in the Burnley goal then made a fine save from Shea as the Clarets' defence came under pressure from the Rovers front-line. The home side went ahead in the most unusual fashion when Burnley defender THORPE put through his own goal from fully 20 yards, his well-hit back pass leaving Dawson flat-footed!

Just before the interval, Duckworth handled Mosscrop's deep cross and BOYLE undeterred by his previous penalty miss, placed the spot-kick hard and low to Robinson's right.

Though both goals led a charmed life in the second half, the deciding goal came just five minutes from time when MOSSCROP cut in from the left to rifle home a powerful shot into the roof of the Rovers net. The Burnley winger almost repeated the feat two minutes later but the Rovers 'keeper brought off a memorable save.

In spite of a missed penalty, the Clarets twice came from behind to take the points in a well contested game.

Blackburn Rovers
A. Robinson; R. Walmsley; F. Duckworth; A. Walmsley; P. Smith; T. Rigg; T. Byrom; D. Shea; P. Dawson; E. Hawksworth; J. Hodkinson

Burnley
J. Dawson; L. Smelt; C. Jones; L. Thorpe; T. Boyle; W. Watson; W. Nesbitt; R. Kelly; W. Taylor; J. Lindsay; E. Mosscrop;

Attendance: 20,000

Match 43
20 September 1919
Burnley 3 Blackburn Rovers 1

In very windy conditions, Rovers had the better of the early play, Eddleston hitting the post before HAWKSWORTH charged down Jones' weak clearance to shoot past Dawson. The visitors continued to press forward and after Hawksworth had brought a fine save out of the Clarets 'keeper, Jones was forced to head off the line when Holland's header had all but beaten Dawson.

At the other end, Crabtree saved well from Lindsay and again when Freeman looked certain to score from Mosscrop's centre. Just before half-time Burnley drew level, it has to be said, against the run of play, when KELLY's long-range shot went in off Crabtree's right-hand post.

However, the second half was dominated by the home side and they took the lead as early as the 49th minute when FREEMAN, taking the ball from Lindsay, shot home, the ball striking the inside of the post before entering the net. The Clarets went further ahead after 66 minutes when Mosscrop worked his way to the by-line before pulling the ball back for NESBITT to smash home.

Crabtree then made good saves from Lindsay and Watson before Nesbitt's first-time shot rattled the crossbar with the Rovers 'keeper well beaten.

Towards the end of the game, Rovers had a couple of chances to reduce the arrears but found Boyle and Watson at the heart of the Clarets defence in outstanding form.

Burnley
J. Dawson; L. Smelt; C. Jones; L. Thorpe; T. Boyle; W. Watson; W. Nesbitt; R. Kelly; B. Freeman; J. Lindsay; E. Mosscrop

Blackburn Rovers
J. Crabtree; W. Dennis; F. Duckworth; T. Rigg; P. Smith; J. Kerr; P. Holland; J. Eddleston; P. Dawson; E. Hawksworth; J. Hodkinson;

Attendance: 20,000

Match 44
15 January 1921
Burnley 4 Blackburn Rovers 1

Before the game got underway, a little diversion was caused by the antics of a monkey running loose in the goalmouth at the cricket field end of Turf Moor!

Owing to the thaw succeeding a frost, the surface of the ground was soft and greasy and this undoubtedly led to the number of mistakes that were made. After a quiet opening quarter-of-an-hour the game burst into life when CROSS receiving possession from Weaver, let fly from fully 25 yards, the ball beating Sewell's frantic dive, to give the Clarets the lead. Cross went close on a couple of occasions as Burnley increased the tempo before Rovers full-back Bibby got in the way of a Kelly piledriver. Every now and again, the Rovers threatened and eventually after 38 minutes, they drew level when Smelt's attempted clearance struck Boyle on the back and bounced kindly for SANDHAM to blast home. Two minutes before half-time, Burnley's lead was restored when KELLY shot home from the edge of the penalty area, though Sewell did get his finger-tips to the ball.

Burnley had the better of the play after the resumption. Kelly was clean through when he was upended by Reilly just outside the penalty area but Anderson wasted the free-kick. Dawson was called into action on a couple of occasions with Thorpe bringing two good saves out of the Burnley 'keeper.

Midway through the second half, Burnley went 3-1 up when following good work by Watson, who beat three Rovers defenders in a mazy dribble, CROSS fired home his second goal of the game. The Clarets' fourth goal came in the 77th minute as BOYLE sent in a magnificent long-shot which beat Sewell's despairing dive and entered the net via the underside of the bar. The home side continued to press forward in search of further goals though their cause wasn't helped when Weaver badly sprained his ankle on the treacherous surface, leaving the Clarets to play the last few minutes with ten men.

Burnley
J. Dawson; L. Smelt; C. Jones; G. Halley; T. Boyle; W. Watson; W. Nesbitt; R. Kelly; J. Anderson; B. Cross; W. Weaver

Blackburn Rovers
R. Sewell; J. Donnelly; E. Bibby; L. Thorpe; F. Reilly; T. Heaton; J. Hodkinson; P. Holland; W. Sandham; E. Hawksworth; S. McCall;

Attendance: 41,534

Match 45
22 January 1921
Blackburn Rovers 1 Burnley 3

Burnley's victory in this East Lancashire Derby was their twenty-first consecutive league match without defeat!

Though playing against a strong breeze in the first half, it was Burnley's Anderson who had the game's first chance but his shot was charged down by Rollo who then sliced his attempted clearance for a corner. Thorpe then kicked clear as Cross shaped to shoot before Rovers' first attack of the game was nullified by a neat interception from Boyle. The game was ten minutes old when Nesbitt was fouled near the corner flag. Halley took the free-kick and KELLY with a well-placed header beat Sewell in the Rovers goal. The first real shot by a Rovers player came from Sandham, when his effort from the edge of the Burnley penalty area grazed the Clarets' crossbar. Hodkinson seemed to have the goal at his mercy but centred instead of shooting! At the other end, Cross cleverly beat Rollo but his first shot was knocked down and his second struck the side netting. Burnley were soon on the attack again and Cross had another goalscoring opportunity, only to have the ball taken off his toes by Duckworth. Rovers equalised in the 38th minute when HODKINSON gave Dawson no chance with a well-struck drive from 25 yards. Just before half-time, MOSSCROP restored the visitors' lead and though he appeared to be offside, the referee allowed the goal, later explaining that he thought the Burnley winger had been played onside.

Early in the second half, Dawson saved well from Sandham but Rovers were soon down to ten men as Healless had to leave the field after injuring his head while heading the ball! After his return, Rovers made all the running and both Hawksworth and Sandham had chances to equalise. However, with just five minutes to play, Burnley scored a third goal, though there was a certain element of luck about it. Watson sent in a hard shot which knocked the luckless Healless unconscious and before the referee could stop the game, ANDERSON pounced on the ball and scored with a fine piece of opportunism.

Blackburn Rovers
R. Sewell; D. Rollo; F. Duckworth; L. Thorpe; H. Healless; J. Kerr; P. Holland; W. Sandham; P. Dawson; E. Hawksworth; J. Hodkinson;

Burnley
J. Dawson; L. Smelt; C. Jones; G. Halley; T. Boyle; W. Watson; W. Nesbitt; R. Kelly; J. Anderson; B. Cross; E. Mosscrop

Attendance: 43,000

Match 46
4 February 1922
Blackburn Rovers 3 Burnley 2

Despite the wintry conditions, both teams served up an excellent game of football. There was an abundance of thrills, five goals scored and many more prevented by two outstanding goalkeepers.

There is no doubt that the opening half-hour belonged to Burnley who not only scored two goals courtesy of Joe Anderson but also rattled the Rovers woodwork on three occasions. The Clarets' first goal came as a result of Reilly's mis-hit back pass, which fell short of Sewell allowing ANDERSON to nip in and steer the ball into the unguarded net. Burnley extended their lead shortly afterwards when Wylie's intelligent through ball caught the Rovers defence off-guard and ANDERSON raced through to score his and Burnley's second goal.

Whether Burnley then became over-confident or just under-estimated the home side, there was a remarkable change in the game.

From hardly venturing into the Burnley half, Rovers attacked incessantly and were rewarded when Dawson's shot was deflected and dropped in the snow for RODGERS to dash in and score with ease! Anderson could have completed his hat-trick on the stroke of half-time but missed the ball which ran through to Cross who brought a fine save out of Sewell. As the referee blew for half-time, RODGERS headed past Dawson in the Burnley goal but despite the appeals by the Clarets defenders that the whistle had gone, the official allowed the goal to stand.

Before the crowd had settled down at the start of the second half, Rovers had gone ahead when Jerry Dawson failed to hold a high looping cross from Thorpe and Percy DAWSON scrambled the ball over the line.

Dawson certainly atoned for his error with the third goal, making a number of breathtaking saves from McIntyre and Hodkinson in particular whilst at the other end, Sewell saved at the feet of Nesbitt as the Clarets went in search of the equaliser.

Blackburn Rovers
R. Sewell; D. Rollo; T. Wylie; J. Forrest; F. Reilly; L. Thorpe; W. Longmuir; N. Rodgers; P. Dawson; J. McIntyre; J. Hodkinson

Burnley
J. Dawson; L. Smelt; D. Taylor; A. Bassnett; T. Boyle; W. Watson; W. Nesbitt; R. Kelly; J. Anderson; B. Cross; E. Mosscrop

Attendance: 20,000

Match 47
11 February 1922
Burnley 1 Blackburn Rovers 2

It was only following an earlier inspection by the referee that Burnley's frozen Turf Moor ground was deemed playable, though it seemed to give the players more trouble than the snow-crusted pitch at Ewood Park.

The home side had the better of the first half in terms of territorial advantage but Sewell in the Blackburn goal wasn't called upon to make a difficult save as the Clarets forwards either shot tamely straight into his hands or missed the target completely. Rovers took the lead against the run of play when Dawson in the Burnley goal misjudged the flight of Longmuir's cross and his namesake Percy DAWSON, leading the line for the visitors, cracked the ball into the back of the net. Towards half-time, the home side's wing-half Halley fell awkwardly on the rock-hard turf and was stretchered off with torn ligaments. His absence not only reduced Burnley to ten men but also seemed to disorganise the whole team. However, just on the stroke of half-time, Kelly hit the woodwork with Sewell well beaten.

Midway through the second half, the ten men of Burnley drew level when Joe ANDERSON shot past an unsighted Sewell. Thorpe led the complaints to the referee stating that the Clarets Scottish-born forward had controlled the ball with his hand before firing home.

Both sides went in search of the winner but it was Blackburn Rovers RODGERS who was the first to find the net as Tommy Boyle delayed his clearance.

The Clarets could claim that they were dogged by bad luck having to play two-thirds of the game with ten men, but in all honesty it was defensive lapses that brought about their downfall.

Burnley
J. Dawson; L. Smelt; D. Taylor; G. Halley; T. Boyle; W. Watson; W. Nesbitt; R. Kelly; J. Anderson; B. Cross; W. Weaver

Blackburn Rovers
R. Sewell; D. Rollo; T. Wylie; H. Healless; F. Reilly; L. Thorpe; W. Longmuir; N. Rodgers; P. Dawson; J. McIntyre; J. Hodkinson

Attendance: 40,919

Match 48
21 October 1922
Burnley 3 Blackburn Rovers 1

Playing with a strong wind at their backs, Burnley made all the early running. Kelly sent Weaver away and whilst the Rovers were appealing for offside, the Clarets winger fired in a swerving shot which Davies did well to turn over the bar. Kelly was instrumental in setting up most of the home side's attacks as the Clarets dominated the first half. The England international flicked the ball to Cross who looked like scoring when he had his legs taken from under him by Walmsley. The resultant penalty-kick taken by KELLY left Davies helpless.

Burnley's second goal came five minutes before the interval when Weaver made ground down the right before crossing for Anderson. Davies did well to get down low to his right to save but he couldn't hold the ball and CROSS followed up to force it home. Though Rovers began the second half with the wind behind them, it was Burnley who continued to do most of the attacking. Davies made a brilliant save from Cross after good work by Weaver, then Anderson headed into the side-netting after Taylor's accurate cross had picked him out.

In a rare Rovers attack, McINTYRE reduced the arrears, firing home from the edge of the area after good approach work by McKay and Bond. The goal seemed to inspire the visitors and Dawson soon had the chance to show his ability, touching Hodkinson's rasping drive over the bar.

Burnley responded in fine style and KELLY netted his second goal of the match. After playing the ball out to Mosscrop, the Clarets inside-right made ground into the six-yard box where he headed the wingers pin-point cross past Davies. In the remaining minutes, Burnley continued to do all the pressing, the Rovers being completely outclassed.

Burnley
J. Dawson; L. Smelt; D. Taylor; H. Gee; A. Bassnett; W. Watson; W. Weaver; R. Kelly; J. Anderson; B. Cross; E. Mosscrop

Blackburn Rovers
E. Davies; R. Walmsley; T. Wylie; H. Healless; F. Reilly; T. Williamson; R. Bond; J. McKay; J. McIntyre; R. Haworth; J. Hodkinson

Attendance: 29,000

Match 49
28 October 1922
Blackburn Rovers 2 Burnley 1

Burnley centre-forward Joe Anderson had the opportunity to score a hat-trick in the opening ten minutes of the match but he failed to take any of the chances that came his way. However, it was the Rovers who took the lead midway through the first half when DAWSON beat his name-sake from the edge of the penalty area, curling a shot into the top left-hand corner of the Burnley 'keeper's net.

The Clarets almost equalised minutes later when a determined run by Weaver took him into the Rovers penalty area where his powerful shot beat Davies but was deflected behind for a corner off Rollo. Kelly, too, made a powerful run but lost control of the ball as he shaped to shoot. Rovers were extremely unlucky not to score a second goal just before half-time, when McIntyre beat Smelt and Taylor before sending in a low drive. Dawson threw himself full length but the ball hit the foot of the upright before Bassnett cleared the danger.

During the early stages of the second half, Dawson came near to scoring a second goal for the home side. After beating Smelt, the Rovers centre-forward overran the ball, allowing Dawson to dive bravely at his feet. Rovers went further ahead in the 52nd minute when Hodkinson centred and McKay turned the ball back to an unmarked BOND who drove it into the roof of the net.

Rovers continued to attack and Dawson was forced into making exceptional saves from both McKay and Hodkinson. In a rare Clarets attack, ANDERSON tried his luck from fully 30 yards, the ball squeezing under Davies' body and hitting the inside of the post before nestling in the back of the net.

In the last few minutes, Blackburn should have gone further ahead but once again Dawson was equal to the task, tipping McKay's thunderous drive onto the bar. Hodkinson seized on the rebound and shot hard before the Burnley 'keeper had time to recover but again the ball struck the upright before Emerson cleared!

Blackburn Rovers
E. Davies; D. Rollo; T. Wylie; H. Heailess; T. Williamson; J. McKinnell; R. Bond; J. McKay; P. Dawson; J. McIntyre; J. Hodkinson

Burnley
J. Dawson; L. Smelt; D. Taylor; W. Emerson; A. Bassnett; W. Watson; W. Weaver; R. Kelly; J. Anderson; B. Cross; E. Mosscrop

Attendance: 23,000

Match 50
3 November 1923
Blackburn Rovers 1 Burnley 1

Ted Harper the Rovers centre-forward shot just over the bar in the opening minute of the game and then a few minutes later put in another powerful drive which Dawson had to tip over to save. From the corner, Dawson saved easily but was pulled up for carrying and a free-kick was awarded just yards from the goal-line. Nothing came of it but Rovers were soon back on the attack with McKinnell forcing the Burnley 'keeper into another outstanding save. Harper missed a golden opportunity to open the scoring when he slipped with only Dawson to beat. Rovers maintained the pressure and Dawson had to save three times in quick succession just before half-time.

After the interval, the game was still one-sided but this time it was the Clarets who were the superior team. Cross was without doubt the best forward on view but it was the combined efforts of Bennie and Kelly that were largely responsible for the tables being so completely turned.

Kelly came close to scoring on a number of occasions but all of his efforts on goal passed narrowly wide. Sewell was forced into action on the hour mark when Hill's header from a Waterfield free-kick forced the Blackburn 'keeper to tip the ball behind for a corner. It was from this corner-kick that Burnley took the lead, Cross supplying KELLY with an inch-perfect pass that left the Clarets inside-forward with the simple task of side-footing the ball home at the far post.

It didn't seem likely that the Rovers would equalise but they did with the game in its last minute. Smelt fouled Byers and a free-kick was awarded. Following a goalmouth scramble, McKAY headed home from close-range and though Dawson made a brave attempt to save, he only succeeded in helping the ball over the line!

Blackburn Rovers
R. Sewell; D. Rollo; T. Wylie; H. Healless; S. Dixon; J. McKinnell; J. Crisp; J. McIntyre; E. Harper; J. McKay; J. Byers

Burnley
J. Dawson; L. Smelt; D. Taylor; A. Bassnett; J. Hill; W. Watson; P. Bennie; R. Kelly; S. Sims; B. Cross; G. Waterfield

Attendance: 20,000

Match 51
10 November 1923
Burnley 1 Blackburn Rovers 2

Burnley had the better of the opening exchanges with Rovers rarely having an opportunity to attack. Eventually however, Harper put in a great shot from 20 yards, which Dawson had to turn round the post. Shortly afterwards with 17 minutes on the clock, the Clarets took the lead. Bennie tricked McKinnell nicely but instead of trying a shot himself, unselfishly laid the ball into the path of BEEL who breasted into the net. Harper was given an opportunity to equalise when Smelt miskicked but he was unable to take advantage of it.

Burnley spent the rest of the half camped in the Rovers half and after Beel's shot had beaten Sewell but hit the post, Kelly put the rebound into the side-netting!

After the restart, Rovers became more of an attacking force and equalised after just four minutes of the second period. Byers' shot appeared to be going wide but HARPER threw himself forward to send in a powerful header that Dawson could do little about. Rovers took the lead in the 51st minute when McINTYRE, receiving the ball at waist height and with his back to goal, scored with a magnificent bicycle kick, though he was probably as surprised as anyone when it came off!

The Clarets then went all out for the equaliser with Waterfield and Kelly having shots turned round the post by the ever-alert Sewell. It seemed only a matter of time before Burnley would draw level but despite the continuous bombardment, the Rovers held out to take the points.

Burnley
J. Dawson; L. Smelt; D. Taylor; A. Bassnett; J. Hill; W. Watson; P. Bennie; R. Kelly; G. Beel; B. Cross; G. Waterfield

Blackburn Rovers
R. Sewell; D. Rollo; T. Wylie; J. Roscamp; T. Williamson; J. McKinnell; J. Crisp; J. McIntyre; E. Harper; J. McKay; J. Byers

Attendance: 30,000

Match 52
13 September 1924
Burnley 3 Blackburn Rovers 5

Burnley should have taken the lead as early as the second minute when Kelly, receiving the ball from Bassnett, raced down the wing before crossing for Freeman to head the ball into the path of George Beel. The Clarets centre-forward hit the ball first time straight into the hands of Sewell, when in fact he had much more time than he thought and could, if he had brought the ball under control, picked his spot!

At the other end, McKay dallied on the ball allowing Smelt to come along and take it off his toes and then shortly afterwards, Evans cleared off the line from Harper's header. It was some time before Rovers broke through the Clarets ranks again as the home side began to score goals.

Parkin put Beel in possession but as he had his back to goal, he laid the ball in the path of HILL whose shot was so well-hit that though Sewell got his hands to it, he couldn't prevent it entering the net. That was after 11 minutes and, only three minutes later, HILL scored his and Burnley's second goal when heading home a Waterfield corner. Burnley went 3-0 up in the 16th minute when Waterfield cut inside two Rovers defenders before crossing for FREEMAN to head over the outstretched arms of Ronnie Sewell.

Within a minute, Rovers had pulled a goal back when McKAY's thunderous shot from Crisp's pass hit the underside of the bar before nestling in the back of Dawson's net. Harper was clean through on goal but with only Dawson to beat, he shot narrowly wide, whilst Healless the Rovers captain forced the Burnley 'keeper into making a full length save from his quickly taken free-kick. Beel the Burnley centre-forward had the ball in the net but much to the disgust of the home crowd, it was disallowed for offside. A minute before half-time, McINTYRE burst through the Clarets defence and his shot hit the crossbar before bouncing down and being kicked clear by Dawson. However, the referee was up with play and he deemed the ball had crossed the line and awarded a goal.

Rovers continued to press forward in the second half and their endeavours were rewarded in the 54th minute when HULME scored after good work by McIntyre. McINTYRE himself put Rovers in the lead ten minutes later when he latched on to Beel's attempted back pass and rounded Dawson before slotting the ball into an empty net. Burnley's misery continued for in the 80th minute, McINTYRE completed his hat-trick to seal the greatest comeback in the history of the East Lancashire Derby.

Burnley
J. Dawson; L. Smelt; J. Evans; A. Bassnett; J. Hill; G. Parkin; R. Kelly;
B. Cross; G. Beel; A. Freeman; G. Waterfield

Blackburn Rovers
R. Sewell; R. Roxburgh; T. Wylie; J. Roscamp; H. Healless; A. Campbell;
J. Hulme; J. McKay; E. Harper; J. McIntyre; J. Crisp

Attendance: 16,000

Match 53
17 January 1925
Blackburn Rovers 0 Burnley 3

When Burnley visited Ewood Park for this East Lancashire derby, only four players occupied the positions they were in when the teams met last September but it made little difference as the Clarets dominated the proceedings.

The visitors took the lead after only three minutes when Kelly played a one-two with Cross before crossing for ROBERTS to head past Sewell at the near post. Burnley went close three minutes later when Hill followed through to take Kelly's pass but his powerful drive cannoned off an opponent for a corner. Tonner then headed against the crossbar and though Beel following up, shot past Sewell, the effort was disallowed for offside. Rollo headed off the line from a Kelly free-kick and had to receive treatment as the force of the shot left him stunned. There was little respite for the harassed Blackburn defence and the only time Dawson in the Burnley goal was called upon in the first half was to deal with a fast rising shot from Crisp. Burnley extended their lead three minutes before the interval when CROSS's 25-yard shot took a deflection off the head of Wylie to leave Sewell completely wrong-footed.

Soon after the restart, the Rovers were awarded a penalty when Crisp was brought down by Parkin as he was clean through the Clarets defence. McKay usually deadly from 12 yards, placed his kick to Dawson's right but the Burnley 'keeper dived to turn the ball round the post.

The Clarets went 3-0 up in the 63rd minute when ROBERTS netted his second goal of the afternoon but once again he was indebted to the work of England international Bob Kelly who beat three Rovers defenders before squaring the ball to the centre-forward.

McIntyre did get the ball in the Burnley net but he was adjudged offside as was Beel whose downward header in the final minute of the game also beat Dawson!

Blackburn Rovers
R. Sewell; D. Rollo; T. Wylie; J. Roscamp; A. Pool; A. Campbell; J. Hulme; J. Crisp; E. Harper; J. McKay; J. McIntyre

Burnley
J. Dawson; A. Fergus; G. Waterfield; J. Hill; J. Armitage; G. Parkin; R. Kelly; B. Cross; W. Roberts; G. Beel; J. Tonner

Attendance: 20,000

Match 54
31 October 1925
Burnley 1 Blackburn Rovers 3

A free-kick awarded against Rovers wing-half Campbell for a clumsy challenge on Page led to Crawford coming under pressure from a hefty challenge by Cross in the opening minute of the game. Bruton cut in from the right and set up a chance for Kelly but his shot was deflected behind for a corner. Cross sent in a powerful 30-yard shot that shaved the outside of Crawford's right-hand post whilst Harper unaccountably shot over the bar from close-range after good work by McIntyre.

The first half ended goalless and, though Crawford was called into action a number of times in the opening stages of the second period, it was Blackburn Rovers who took the lead. The goal after 62 minutes came from the boot of Ted HARPER who completely caught Dawson in the Burnley goal unaware, shooting home from 25 yards when the Clarets defence was expecting a cross.

Burnley pressed hard in search of an equaliser and Beel was hurt as he challenged Crawford for a Bruton cross. Rovers extended their lead six minutes from time when HARPER headed home Hulme's pin-point cross, though there was a suspicion of offside. Three minutes later, Hulme and HARPER repeated the performance as the Rovers centre-forward completed his hat-trick.

Within a minute, Burnley had pulled a goal back as Kelly's cross was met by PAGE whose first-time shot gave Crawford no chance. In the last minute, Page cut inside Rollo and let fly from the edge of the area but Crawford was equal to the task, though he was beaten by the last kick of the game when Cross side-footed Kelly's cross inches wide of the post.

Burnley
J. Dawson; A. McCluggage; G. Waterfield; A. Bassnett; J. Hill; L. Hughes; J. Bruton; B. Cross; R. Kelly; G. Beel; L. Page

Blackburn Rovers
J. Crawford; D. Rollo; R. Roxburgh; J. Roscamp; H. Healless; A. Campbell; J. Hulme; S. Puddefoot; E. Harper; J. McIntyre; A. Rigby

Attendance: 26,181

Match 55
13 March 1926
Blackburn Rovers 6 Burnley 3

With Burnley fighting desperately to avoid relegation and Rovers not yet out of the danger zone, the encounter between these two East Lancashire rivals was fraught to say the least. Both sides were without their regular centre-half with Harry Healless (Rovers) and James Hill (Burnley) playing for the Football League and Scottish League respectively.

The defences were certainly on top in the early stages of the game and the first real shot came from Rovers wing-half McKinnell who forced Dawson to turn the ball over the bar. Burnley, too, came close when Beel crossed for Roberts but the Clarets centre-forward headed straight at Sewell. Quick end-to-end raids were the order of the day and a misunderstanding between Steel and Dawson gave Rigby a gilt-edged opening but he shot wide. Twice Page skimmed the Rovers' crossbar with long-range efforts whilst at the other end, Puddefoot failed to make the most of a one-on-one with Dawson. The Burnley 'keeper then made a wonderful one-handed save from a Ted Harper header but could do little from the resulting corner as PUDDEFOOT headed home from close-in. In the closing minute of the first half, Sewell was beaten three times but, on each occasion, a defender popped up on the goal-line to clear the danger.

Four minutes into the second half, Beel had the ball in the Rovers' net but the 'goal' was disallowed, Roberts having handled. RIGBY then extended the home side's lead after missing a couple of easier chances, crashing home Crisp's centre. The goal seemed to take the sting out of the Burnley attack and Dawson had to fist away a curling shot from Mitchell. A third goal was not long in coming as RIGBY's shot was deflected by McCluggage past the wrong-footed Dawson. A fourth goal came within seconds as PUDDEFOOT crowned a superb solo effort with a drive that almost burst the net!

As Rovers eased up, Burnley pulled a goal back in the 80th minute,

RICHARDS heading in from a corner. Shortly afterwards, Harper missed an open goal but RIGBY scored his third and Rovers' fifth with a close-range shot. A minute later the deficit was further reduced as RICHARDS netted his and Burnley's second, turning in Steel's cross. Two minutes from time, HARPER controlled a long through-ball from Mitchell and shot past the advancing Dawson. Even then, Puddefoot almost added another but his shot brought the save of the game out of the Burnley 'keeper. With the referee poised to blow for full-time, BRUTON scored a third for Burnley.

Blackburn Rovers
R. Sewell; D. Rollo; H. Jones; J. McKinnell; A. Campbell; J. McIntyre; J. Crisp; S. Puddefoot; E. Harper; A. Rigby; T. Mitchell

Burnley
J. Dawson; A. McCluggage; G. Waterfield; J. Steel; S. Spargo; W. Dougall; J. Bruton; P. Richards; W. Roberts; G. Beel; L. Page

Attendance: 29,991

Match 56
16 October 1926
Blackburn Rovers 1 Burnley 5

The Clarets went a goal up after just four minutes of this highly-charged East Lancashire Derby. Hill won the ball in the middle of the park and fed Bruton whose pin-point centre was easily converted by CROSS. Rovers wasted a chance to equalise moments later when Puddefoot receiving the ball from McIntyre was well off the mark with a high shot. Still the home forwards kept up the pressure on the Burnley goal but Puddefoot again disappointed by shooting wide. McCluggage was the forced to clear the ball hastily over his own bar whilst from the resulting corner, McIntyre's first-time shot scraped Sommerville's bar. At the other end, Cross sent in a powerful shot which Cope, in the Rovers goal, needed two attempts in saving. Page almost extended the Clarets' lead but after going past both Roscamp and Hutton, shot tamely wide. Rovers equalised in the 36th minute completely against the run of play. The goal came from a free-kick for a foul by Waterfield on Harper. Rigby's well-struck free-kick was too powerful for Sommerville to hold and PUDDEFOOT following up scored from an acute angle. Healless then headed out from under his own crossbar as the visitors continued to push forward. There was an unusual occurrence at the start of the second half for the players had been lined up ready for the restart before the officials appeared after prolonged vociferous whistling from the good humoured crowd!

Burnley almost took the lead in the opening minute of the second half, for after Hutton had handled Page's centre, Bruton's free-kick hit the foot of Cope's left-hand post. Beel then missed the easiest chance of the match before Page headed against the crossbar. The Clarets winger then beat both Roscamp and Jones before forcing Cope into making a brilliant save. The game looked to be heading for a draw with just nine minutes to play. Page was brought down by Hutton and the referee had no hesitation in awarding a penalty. McCLUGGAGE made no mistake from the spot, after which the Clarets ran riot. Within two minutes, FREEMAN netted from close-range following good work by Page and then a minute later, PAGE rounded Hutton and fired an unstoppable shot out of Cope's reach. The Clarets scored again in the final minute as PAGE headed home Bruton's accurate cross to complete the rout – their four goals late in the second-half coming in the space of eight minutes!

Blackburn Rovers
H. Cope; J. Hutton; H. Jones; J. Roscamp; H. Healless; J. McIntyre; J. Walter; S. Puddefoot; E. Harper; J. McKay; A. Rigby

Burnley
G. Sommerville; A. McCluggage; G. Waterfield; J. Steel; J. Hill; W. Dougall; J. Bruton; B. Cross; G. Beel; A. Freeman; L. Page

Attendance: 42,289

Match 57
5 March 1927
Burnley 3 Blackburn Rovers 1

For the first time since the 1922-23 season, Burnley succeeded in beating Blackburn Rovers at Turf Moor and as they won at Ewood Park in October, completed the 'double' over their old rivals.

Heavy rain had turned the ground into something resembling a swamp. The surface was covered with water and it was not at all conducive to good play. Nevertheless, the players on both sides conquered the adverse conditions to serve up a fast and exciting game. Burnley had the better of the first half but their finishing left a lot to be desired. Page was a real live-wire and all the danger came from his speedy runs and centres but it was not made the most of by his team-mates. The Clarets' first goal came as a result of a foul on Page by Roxburgh. Dougall dropped the free-kick on to BEEL's head and he gave Crawford no chance from six yards out.

Twice Harper came close to levelling the scores before Sommerville miskicked in the area, presenting Rigby with a simple chance that he failed to take. Beel did get the ball in the Rovers net but he was well offside. Rovers eventually got on level terms thanks to a free-kick that was splendidly converted by CAMPBELL. The visitors pressed forward in search of a second goal and had Puddefoot been more alert, they would surely have taken the lead. The Burnley goal had another escape when Holland hit the upright with the Clarets' defence well beaten. McKay was brought down in the area by Steel but the referee refused Rovers a penalty. After 22 minutes, CROSS gave Burnley the lead after which it was all one-way traffic. BEEL netted a third for the Clarets after Roxburgh's tackled failed to halt his run.

There was no further scoring in the second half as McCluggage and Waterfield defended stubbornly at the heart of the Burnley defence – Rovers best chance fell to Puddefoot whose blistering shot was well saved by Sommerville.

Burnley
G. Sommerville; A. McCluggage; G. Waterfield; J. Steel; J. Hill; W. Dougall; J. Bruton; B. Cross; G. Beel; J. Devine; L. Page

Blackburn Rovers
J. Crawford; R. Roxburgh; H. Jones; J. Roscamp; H. Healless; A. Campbell; S. Puddefoot; D. Holland; E. Harper; J. McKay; A. Rigby;

Attendance: 24,546

Match 58
27 August 1927
Blackburn Rovers 2 Burnley 1

When clubs like Blackburn Rovers and Burnley are in opposition, there is inevitably more than the customary excitement in the air. This meeting on the opening day of the season was watched by a crowd of 32,441 who saw an exciting game, not because of the high quality of football but because of the speed and enthusiasm of both sides.

The game was crammed with incident from start to finish and the result in doubt right to the end.

The Clarets took the lead in the 34th minute when HARGREAVES latched on to a poor throw-in by Healless to shoot past the advancing

Crawford. The Burnley forward almost increased his side's lead moments later when his shot beat Crawford all ends up, only for Hutton to clear spectacularly off the goal-line.

Early in the second half, Rovers equalised when PUDDEFOOT's cross came back off the bar. Both Harper and Sommerville jumped for the ball but neither touched it and though Burnley's Jimmy Hill tried desperately to clear the danger he only succeeded in kicking the ball, which was already over the line, into the roof of the net!

Burnley went straight to the other end and after a miskick by Rankin, Crawford brought off a fine save from Haddow's snap shot.

Rovers' second goal came just four minutes after their opener. Walter centred for McLEAN to meet the ball as it dropped and he hit it on the volley past a startled Sommerville.

Afterwards, Harper came close on two occasions as Rovers maintained their superiority, though there always remained the danger of a Burnley breakaway.

Blackburn Rovers
J. Crawford; J. Hutton; H. Jones; H. Healless; W. Rankin; J. Whyte; J. Walter; S. Puddefoot; E. Harper; T. McLean; A. Rigby

Burnley
G. Sommerville; A. Reid; G. Waterfield; G. Parkin; J. Hill; W. Dougall; J. Bruton; J. Devine; A. Haddow; H. Hargreaves; L. Page

Attendance: 32,441

Match 59
31 December 1927
Burnley 3 Blackburn Rovers 1

The recent success of Blackburn Rovers prompted quite a big contingent of fans to travel by road and rail, though the railway company was caught napping as quite a large number of Rovers fans had to have their money returned because there was no train available to take them!

Unfortunately, the Arctic weather went a long way to spoiling the occasion. Not only was it cold, the light was bad and the underfoot conditions were such that first-class football was a difficult proposition.

The home side adapted themselves to the conditions much quicker than their opponents. The Clarets swung the ball about freely whilst Rovers were trying to make headway down the middle of the field and so their wingers had little chance to show their ability. Crawford had already made two outstanding saves when he was beaten in the 12th minute by BEEL who seized on to a loose ball in the penalty area after Bruton's cross had only been partially cleared. Nearly all the danger to the Rovers goal came from attacks down Burnley's right flank where Steel, Bruton and Freeman combined well. Burnley extended their lead five minutes before the interval when PAGE met Bruton's pin-point cross to head home.

In the opening minutes of the second half, Mitchell tested Down with a powerful header and then reduced the arrears. It all started with a long ball out of defence by Whyte that appeared to be going out of play. Rovers winger Thornewell gave chase and retrieved the ball near the corner flag before crossing for MITCHELL to head past Down. Rovers pressed hard in search of an equaliser but with just minutes remaining, Hutton was harshly adjudged to have fouled Page and from the resultant penalty, McCLUGGAGE made it 3-1. With virtually the last kick of the game, Rovers were lucky not to concede a fourth goal when Bruton struck the post from Page's centre.

Burnley
W. Down; A. McCluggage; G. Waterfield; J. Steel; J. Hill; G. Parkin; J. Bruton; A. Freeman; G. Beel; P. Dougall; L. Page

Blackburn Rovers
J. Crawford; J. Hutton; H. Jones; H. Healless; A. Campbell; J. Whyte; C. Thornewell; S. Puddefoot; T. Mitchell; T. McLean; A. Rigby

Attendance: 28,354

Match 60
20 October 1928
Burnley 2 Blackburn Rovers 2

This was the first time the clubs had shared the league points at Turf Moor since 1892-93, so the result was not an ordinary one!

Whilst there were some outstanding moves, mostly by Rovers, there were some blunders both in passing and near the goal, while the ball was far too often out of play.

It was a greasy surface that caused the mistakes to be made and both Beel and Page missed golden opportunities to open the scoring, the openings being presented to them within minutes of each other. Burnley should have taken the lead midway through the first half but Hill shot over with the Rovers goal unguarded.

Roscamp threw away one chance of opening the scoring, hesitating with only Down to beat but then McLEAN gave the visitors the lead, heading home a deep cross by Thornewell. The Rovers forward increased his sides lead when fastening on to a fine through ball from Campbell and side-footing past the advancing Down.

Burnley pulled a goal back early in the second half when McCLUGGAGE netted from the penalty-spot following a harsh decision of handball against Jones. His first attempt was brilliantly saved by Crawford but the referee ordered the kick to be retaken after Rovers players had encroached into the area. This time the Burnley full-back made no mistake, firing high into the roof of the net. By now, DEVINE who had to leave the field after a clash of heads had returned but was playing out of position. It was he who secured the Clarets a point when he rather fortuitously deflected a ball that was going out of play to completely deceive Crawford in the Rovers goal.

The closing stages when both teams were fighting hard to secure the winning goal were fraught with much excitement, the nearest either side came to breaking the deadlock coming from Burnley's George Beel who brought a magnificent save out of Crawford.

Burnley
W. Down; A. McCluggage; G. Waterfield; J. Steel; J. Hill; G. Parkin; J. Bruton; F. Fitton; G. Beel; J. Devine; L. Page

Blackburn Rovers
J. Crawford; R. Roxburgh; H. Jones; H. Healless; P. O'Dowd; A. Campbell; C. Thornewell; S. Puddefoot; J. Roscamp; T. McLean; A. Rigby

Attendance: 35,694

Match 61
2 May 1929
Blackburn Rovers 1 Burnley 1

Andy McCluggage's failure to convert an 85th-minute penalty-kick awarded for a foul on Louis Page by Baxter, robbed the Clarets of victory in this re-arranged East Lancashire Derby at Ewood Park. Had he succeeded instead of shooting wide, it would have been rather hard on Rovers, for they were quite easily the more aggressive of the sides, particularly in the second half and deserved more than the one point they got.

There was not much between the teams before the interval. Burnley began well and Bruton's clever wing play set up a number of chances, which the visitors' forwards failed to take. Eventually though, Rovers left-back Roxburgh got the measure of the Burnley forward and the visitors chances became far fewer.

There was some erratic shooting by both sides, though Rovers nearly took the lead when Clarrie Bourton pushed the ball out for Keating to send in a first-time shot from the right-hand side of the area against the far upright. Burnley took the lead on the half-hour mark following a misunderstanding in the Rovers defence. Roxburgh played the ball back to Crawford but before he could clear it, BRUTON ran on and placed the ball into the bottom left-hand corner of the net with the Rovers keeper stranded.

Rovers' goal came five minutes from the interval after Bourton and Keating had both struck the bar. Bourton swung the ball across the goalmouth and though Keating fell, PUDDEFOOT dashed in to bundle the ball over the line.

For an end of season game, the play was fast and furious with both sides fully committed to giving their all!

Blackburn Rovers
J. Crawford; T. Baxter; R. Roxburgh; J. Roscamp; W. Rankin; P. O'Dowd; S. Puddefoot; A. Keating; C. Bourton; T. Mitchell; A. Rigby

Burnley
W. Down; W. Knox; A. McCluggage; G. Parkin; S. Bowsher; H. Storer; J. Bruton; W. Stage; G. Beel; J. Devine; L. Page

Attendance: 5,461

Match 62
9 November 1929
Blackburn Rovers 8 Burnley 3

One of the most memorable East Lancashire Derbies certainly brightened up a dismal November afternoon at Ewood Park. The poor weather certainly kept a number of people at home and with both sides under strength, it seemed to be a wise move!

The visitors had the better of the early play with both Page and Mantle going close. However, once McLean began to get more of the ball, his accurate passing started to create gaps in the Clarets' defence. Rovers took the lead in the 25th minute when GROVES received the ball from Imrie and evaded McCluggage's tackle before shooting past Down. Five minutes later, the Clarets were level when Jones and Bruton clashed in the penalty area and the referee awarded a penalty which McCLUGGAGE put away with ease. Almost on the stroke of half-time, Rovers went 2-1 up when ROSCAMP, who looked fractionally offside, headed home Turner's cross. Devine, the Burnley inside-left had spent the last five minutes of the first half off the field injured, but he returned for the start of the second period.

ROSCAMP soon extended Rovers' lead but knew little about it as an attempted clearance from Waterfield hit him and rebounded into the net. There was no doubting the scorer of the home side's fourth goal as McLEAN hit a beautiful 25-yard shot into the top corner of Down's goal. A minute later IMRIE made it 5-1 for Rovers with his first goal for the club, a gloriously struck free-kick.

The Clarets refused to lie down and reduced the arrears through Louis PAGE who volleyed home Bruton's cross. This seemed to spur Rovers on even more and McLEAN and GROVES added two goals in the space of a minute. In the 88th minute, McCLUGGAGE netted his second goal from the penalty-spot before GROVES netted his second and Blackburn's eighth goal in a most convincing win for Rovers over the Clarets.

Blackburn Rovers
J. Crawford; J. Hutton; H. Jones; W. Imrie; W. Rankin; P. O'Dowd; W. Crompton; T. McLean; J. Roscamp; A. Groves; T. Turner

Burnley
W. Down; A. McCluggage; G. Waterfield; J. Brown; S. Bowsher; J. Steel; J. Bruton; J. Wallace; J. Mantle; J. Devine; L. Page

Attendance: 22,647

Match 63
15 March 1930
Burnley 3 Blackburn Rovers 2

Since the first meeting of these clubs earlier in the season, Jack Bruton had left Turf Moor and become a Blackburn Rovers player, while O'Dowd, who was the Ewood club's left-back in the earlier meeting, was Burnley's centre-half, both playing against their former colleagues for the first time.

Wintry conditions with snow falling for most of the game kept the gate down.

Rovers took the lead against the run of play in the 34th minute when McLEAN's shot struck Brown and was deflected into the net out of the reach of Sommerville. Four minutes later, a high centre by Page out near the corner flag, dropped under the bar, the wind having brought it back into play. This deceived BINNS who could only push the ball into his own net. Rovers went 2-1 up in the last minute of the first half when BOURTON fastened on to Cunliffe's cross and hit a hard low drive past Sommerville.

In the first minute of the second half, Burnley were level, courtesy of another McCLUGGAGE penalty. This time it was Rankin who suffered an injustice in being in the way of a hard right foot drive by Page. Though he was able to show the referee the mark on his right chest and shoulder, the official ignored his protest and allowed McCluggage to equalise.

The second half belonged to the Clarets and it was only the excellent goalkeeping of Binns in the Blackburn goal that prevented a much heavier defeat. Burnley's third goal came from the boot of former Rovers favourite O'DOWD who scored direct from a free-kick after Hutton had been adjudged to have brought down Wallace. Despite the one-way traffic of the second half. McLean did have the chance to level things up but shot tamely straight at Sommerville.

Burnley
G. Sommerville; A. McCluggage; G. Waterfield; J. Brown; P. O'Dowd; A. Forrest; J. Mantle; T. Prest; G. Beel; J. Wallace; L. Page

Blackburn Rovers
C. Binns; J. Hutton; H. Jones; W. Imrie; W. Rankin; J. Roscamp; J. Bruton; S. Puddefoot; C. Bourton; T. McLean; A. Cunliffe

Attendance: 16,673

Match 64
24 October 1936
Burnley 0 Blackburn Rovers 0

Following Blackburn Rovers relegation to the Second Division, the clubs met in the first East Lancashire Derby for six years. Despite the heavy drizzle, a crowd of 32,567 was packed into Turf Moor, giving Burnley their biggest home gate in their present spell in Division Two.

Rovers, who had lost heavily against Newcastle United and Barnsley in their last two matches, made seven changes, three of them positional. It was the visitors who started as the better side and Richmond was forced to turn the ball for a corner as Beattie shaped to shoot. Fine play down the right between Whiteside and Bruton led to a goalscoring opportunity for Sale but he screwed his shot wide of the target. The Rovers winger had another chance moments later but delayed his shot, allowing Hubbick to get in a tackle. Just before half-time, Burnley's 'keeper Hetherington only partially cleared a corner but as Beattie shaped to apply a powerful drive, he completely missed his kick!

Burnley's chances were few and far between and it was still Rovers who were having the better of things when the second half got underway. Sale hit the outside of Hetherington's right-hand post and then brought a fine save out of the Burnley 'keeper with a powerful downward header. On the hour mark, Rovers 'keeper Hughes made his only noteworthy save of the match, beating out a fierce shot by Lawton. Hetherington was caught in two minds whether or not to come for a Bruton cross which was met on the volley by Sale. His effort beat the Burnley 'keeper but landed on the roof of the net! Rovers did have the ball in the Burnley net when Bruton curled in a high free-kick that the referee on the advice of the Burnley 'keeper Hetherington deemed had crossed the by-line. However, the ball landed two feet in front of the bar and was knocked into his own goal by the Clarets 'keeper!

Miller for Burnley and Thompson for Rovers both went close in the final few minutes but the game remained goalless.

Burnley
T. Hetherington; G. Richmond; H. Hubbick; J. Hindmarsh; A. Woodruff; A. Robinson; J. Gastall; R. Brocklebank; T. Lawton; W. Miller; J. Stein

Blackburn Rovers
J. Hughes; J. Gorman; W. Crook; A. Whiteside; N. Christie; R. Pryde; J. Bruton; J. Beattie; E. Thompson; P. Gallacher; T. Sale

Attendance: 32,567

Match 65
27 February 1937
Blackburn Rovers 3 Burnley 1

This game was a chilly experience for all the players, in muddy and rain-soaked clothing and having to contend with a heavy ground surface which drained the physical resources of both sides.

Burnley made all the early running with outside-left Fletcher the main threat. Not only did he have the beating of Lanceley but also Crook when he switched flanks. Fletcher almost opened the scoring after ten minutes when his powerful shot was well saved by Hughes in the

Blackburn goal. Lanceley was under so much pressure from Fletcher that on one occasion, he sliced a clearance in front of his own goal on to the roof of the Darwen End!

The Clarets took a deserved lead in the 17th minute when STEIN headed home direct from Fletcher's corner kick. Rovers thought they had equalised a minute later but Butt used his hand to turn the ball into the net from a long high centre by Whiteside. However, Rovers were on level terms after 33 minutes when BUTT sprinted through the Burnley defence and hit a low shot into the corner of the net, well out of Adams' reach.

Rovers stepped up a gear after the interval with Wightman and Butt in the thick of the action. The home side took the lead in the 63rd minute when BRUTON netted against his old club. His shot took a wicked deflection off Robinson, leaving Adams completely wrong-footed. Rovers centre-forward Sale scraped the outside of Adams' right-hand post with a fine overhead kick before GUEST scored the home side's third goal, racing on to Calladine's pass and shooting past the advancing Hughes.

Blackburn Rovers
J. Hughes; E. Lancely; W. Crook; A. Whiteside; R. Pryde; J. Wightman; J. Bruton; L. Butt; T. Sale; C. Calladine; W. Guest

Burnley
E. Adams; G. Richmond; A. Robinson; F. Rayner; A. Woodruff; W. Smith; J. Stein; P. Fisher; J. Gastall; W. Miller; C. Fletcher

Attendance: 18,240

Match 66
11 December 1937
Blackburn Rovers 3 Burnley 3

Half-a-dozen goals, five of them in the second half and two in the last few minutes – Burnley three times in front, Rovers grimly fighting back – those were the ingredients of a game that ended in a draw but might have gone either way! Friday's snowstorm made underfoot conditions treacherous and unpleasant with the result that a fixture expected to attract a bumper attendance, drew a gate of 15,136.

If ever a game belied its early portents, this one did. Rovers opened with a flourish, Mortimer forcing Adams to a good low save, Butt putting a short-range effort against the outside of the post, Bruton having a shot blocked on the line and Pryde beating Adams all ends up only to see his looping header land on the roof of the net.

Burnley gradually clawed their way back into the game and only brilliant goalkeeping by Barron foiled the Clarets forwards, Miller in particular. Barron finger-tipped away a 30-yard drive from the Burnley inside-forward before getting down well to a cross drive by Storey. Burnley eventually took the lead in the 27th minute when MILLER side-stepped Pryde's challenge before slotting the ball past Barron. Robson had two opportunities to extend Burnley's lead before the interval but finished weakly, whilst Brocklebank grazed the Rovers' bar from the edge of the penalty area.

The scores were level five minutes after the interval when BUTT beat Adams with a sharp, rising drive from just inside the box. Another five minutes and Burnley were back in front – Storey was brought down in the penalty area and though Barron got his hands to STEIN's spot-kick, he couldn't prevent the ball entering the net. Rovers equalised on the hour when an unmarked BUTT headed home Dickie's cross. Mortimer broke through but shot straight at Adams. The Burnley 'keeper threw the ball out to Robson who sprinted downfield with the Rovers defence in hot pursuit before crossing to STOREY who left Barron helpless with a low drive. With just a couple of minutes remaining, Crook placed a free-kick well forward and BRUTON atoned for an earlier miss with a half-hit shot that trickled just inside the post for the equaliser.

Blackburn Rovers

J. Barron; F. Hall; W. Crook; A. Whiteside; R. Pryde; C. Calladine; J. Bruton; L. Butt; E. Mortimer; P. Dickie; W. Guest

Burnley

E. Adams; A. Robinson; T. Chester; L. Martindale; R. Johnson; W. Smith; T. Storey; W. Miller; W. Robson; R. Brocklebank; J. Stein

Attendance: 15,136

Match 67
23 April 1938
Burnley 3 Blackburn Rovers 1

The game was only a couple of minutes old when Rovers thought they should have had a penalty. Len Butt had just robbed Robinson and was poised to shoot when the Burnley captain took his legs from under him.

The referee, Jack Botham of Walsall, was probably the only person in the ground who thought the tackle a fair one!

As it was, it was the Clarets who took the lead after twenty minutes following a desperate goal-line clearance by Hall. The ball came out to Stein who worked his way to the by-line before pulling the ball back for BROCKLEBANK to fire home.

Rovers should have equalised a couple of minutes later when Bruton worked a fine opening for Butt but the normally reliable inside-forward missed his kick with only Adams to beat.

In the first minute of the second half, a long cross shot from Guest hit the angle of the goal and rebounded into play. To add to their disappointment, Rovers 'keeper Mattier almost immediately afterwards misjudged a somewhat similar ball from STEIN and allowed it to sneak under the bar. Thus instead of being level, the visitors were 2-0 down.

Stein and Brocklebank both hit the woodwork before BROCKLEBANK got Burnley's third goal thirteen minutes from time. A fine run by Bruton was the preliminary to Rovers' consolation goal scored by GUEST.

A Derby in name only, for once the early indications had been proved false, the football virtues were far too much the possession of one side as Burnley completely outclassed their rivals.

Burnley
E. Adams; A. Robinson; T. Chester; L. Martindale; R. Johnson; F. Rayner; T. Storey; W. Miller; R. Brocklebank; P. Fisher; J. Stein

Blackburn Rovers
G. Mattier; W. Hough; W. Crook; W. Halsall; F. Hall; R. Pryde; J. Bruton; L. Butt; F. Chivers; C. Calladine; W. Guest

Attendance: 14,139

Match 68
15 October 1938
Burnley 3 Blackburn Rovers 2

The Clarets took the lead after only two minutes when Gardner, probably the best player on the field, was unwittingly put in possession by Bobby Langton after he leapt to keep in play a long clearance that he might well have left alone. Gardner made ground and crossed for CLAYTON to side foot home from close-range.

Burnley went 2-0 up in the 17th minute when Gardner cut through the Rovers defence towards the left before switching the ball out to the right. Taylor then hit a deep cross which CLAYTON headed past Barron for both his and the Clarets second goal. Rovers almost pulled a goal back in the dying moments of the first half but Clarke headed inches wide from a good position.

However, CLARKE made amends five minutes into the second half with a fine individual goal. Faced by three Burnley defenders, he took the ball to the left of the penalty area before unleashing an unstoppable drive well out of Adams' reach. Clayton thought he had completed his hat-trick on the hour mark but his conversion of Gardner's cross was deemed offside. Two minutes later, Rovers were level when CLARKE headed his second goal from a deep cross by Butt. Rovers should have taken the lead a minute later but Rogers somehow contrived to scoop the ball over the bar from near the post – a seemingly impossible feat! Then, as Rovers pressed for the winner, another gilt-edged chance was presented to Weddle but from only a yard out, he flicked it past the post!

When the winning goal did come, it came at the other end following a series of errors by the Blackburn defence. Chivers sliced a clearance across goal, Hough and Barron in succession failed to clear the danger and HORNBY gleefully accepted his unexpected chance!

Burnley
E. Adams; A. Robinson; T. Chester; T. Gardner; R. Johnson; G. Bray; F. Taylor; W. Miller; J. Clayton; R. Brocklebank; R. Hornby

Blackburn Rovers
J. Barron; W. Hough; W. Crook; A. Whiteside; R. Pryde; F. Chivers; W. Rogers; L. Butt; J. Weddle; N. Clarke; R. Langton

Attendance: 29,254

Match 69
18 February 1939
Blackburn Rovers 1 Burnley 0

The last League meeting between the two clubs prior to the Second World War was a somewhat dull and uninspiring affair. This was chiefly because Burnley's early sparkle was snuffed out when they lost the services of Billingham their young centre-forward.

It was the Clarets, who in the twenty minutes before Billingham's injury produced the one purple patch of the afternoon. The quickness of their passing and the general sprightliness of their attack prompted by Gardner seemed to suggest a profitable day for the visitors.

The injury came as Bob Pryde tackled Billingham as he was going through, hooking the ball off his toes and coming away cleanly with it. The Clarets striker was obviously in a lot of pain and he was helped over the line for attention. He was then carried from the field and taken to the Blackburn Royal Infirmary for an x-ray examination for a suspected broken ankle – fortunately no bone was broken.

Rovers then began to seize the initiative and just five minutes after Billingham's departure they took the lead. With a free-kick for a foul on Butt by Woodruff, Guest shot into a line of defenders before the ball bounced kindly for ROGERS who placed his shot wide of Adams, just inside the far post.

Afterwards, the home side attacked hard but with little imagination or conviction. They appeared satisfied with the goal they had scored, but it was a small safety margin. Indeed, in the last minute, Taylor rose well to a centre from the Burnley left and his powerful header passed inches over the bar with Barron well beaten!

Blackburn Rovers
J. Barron; W. Hough; W. Crook; A. Whiteside; R. Pryde; F. Chivers; W. Rogers; L. Butt; J. Weddle; R. Langton; W. Guest

Bu rnley
E. Adams; A. Robinson; J. Marshall; T. Gardner; A. Woodruff; G. Bray; F. Taylor; W. Morris; J. Billingham; R. Brocklebank; R. Hornby

Attendance: 30,223

Match 70
9 December 1939
Blackburn Rovers 1 Burnley 0

Within seconds of the kick-off, a good clearance by Mather enabled Hornby to race forward. At the right moment, he passed inside to Knight, whose shot struck the bar. After quarter-of-an-hour, a weak clearance by Pryde let in Clayton whose shot was turned behind by Robinson for a corner.

For a considerable time, both teams indulged in much erratic kicking before Rovers inside-right Higham shot over from point-blank range. Knight had an excellent chance of opening Burnley's account but he hesitated at the last moment, enabling Hough to intervene.

After Blackburn's defence had dealt with two threatening Burnley raids immediately after the resumption, they gained the lead. ROGERS went away nicely on the right wing and after evading Mather's lunging tackle, centred the ball. Bentley in the Burnley goal misjudged its flight and it passed over his head into the net.

Rogers nearly netted his and Blackburn's second goal when after dribbling his way through a crowded penalty area, he shot tamely into the hands of Bentley. Burnley were now defending for long periods and the Clarets 'keeper Bentley parried an effort from Weddle before diving at the feet of McShane. He later saved well from Rogers and Robinson as Rovers went all out for a second goal.

Blackburn Rovers
J. Robinson; W. Hough; W. Crook; A. Whiteside; R. Pryde; F. Chivers; W. Rogers; N. Higham; J. Weddle; J. Wightman; H. McShane

Burnley
G. Bentley; J. Marshall; H. Mather; T. Gardner; A. Woodruff; G. Bray; F. Taylor; R. Brocklebank; J. Clayton; G. Knight; R. Hornby

Attendance: 1,233

Match 71
6 April 1940
Burnley 0 Blackburn Rovers 0

Though the game was goalless, Burnley could have scored as early as the first minute when Gardner's free-kick was met by the head of Bob Brocklebank who flicked it on to Hornby. Although on the blind side of the goal, he crashed the ball inches wide of the target and into the side-netting. The Clarets continued to press forward in search of the opening goal and Brocklebank raced clear of a static Rovers defence only to shoot straight at the advancing Fairbrother. Rovers' narrowest escape came in the 43rd minute when Smith pushed the ball to the unmarked Brocklebank ten yards out but with only Fairbrother to beat, he shot over the bar.

Early in the second half, Burnley lost their goalkeeper Morton, who in diving at the feet of the on-rushing Cahill, sustained a serious leg injury and was forced to leave the field. The versatile Smith donned the green jersey and though he was not quite as orthodox as goalkeepers should be, he was very effective – if, on occasions, a little fortunate!

At the other end, Fairbrother was still the busier of the two goalkeepers, saving well from both Brocklebank and Knight.

Smith tipped over the bar from Briscoe before amusing the spectators with one clearance. Woodruff was harassed by Cahill and Gardner and passed back to the Clarets stand-in 'keeper. Rather than pick up the ball, he took a lusty kick at it and sent it one bounce over Fairbrother's goal!

Burnley
J. Morton; J. Marshall; H. Mather; T. Gardner; A. Woodruff; G. Bray; T. Smith; B. Wood; R. Brocklebank; G. Knight; R. Hornby

Blackburn Rovers
J. Fairbrother; W. Hough; E. Lancely; A. Whiteside; R. Pryde; F. Chivers; J. Briscoe; P. Dickie; R. Cahill; G. Glaister; R. Hulbert

Attendance: 2,995

Match 72
31 August 1940
Burnley 2 Blackburn Rovers 1

The first real attack of the match was launched by Rovers. From a free-kick, Crook lofted the ball into the Burnley goalmouth where Adams saved well under pressure from Brindle and Cahill. The Clarets, too, had their moments, the best chance falling to Knight, who on receiving the ball from Gardner, cut inside Crook and fired against the legs of Fairbrother.

Rovers took the lead in the 25th minute when following a foul on Cahill, they were awarded a direct free-kick on the edge of the penalty area. Bob PRYDE's powerful, fast rising shot sent the ball into the corner of the net before Adams could move to it. Burnley conceded another free-kick in a similar position minutes later but this time, Pryde's effort was well held by the Clarets 'keeper.

Shortly afterwards, Burnley equalised when Knight's shot rebounded off the foot of the post to the on-rushing HORNBY who netted from close-range.

Early in the second half, Rovers free-kick specialist Bob Pryde was in action again. The kick just outside the penalty area was for an infringement by Woodruff on Hargreaves. Pryde shot narrowly over the bar and when the referee ordered the kick to be re-taken, the Rovers defender cracked the ball against an upright before it was cleared to safety. Shortly after BROCKLEBANK had missed the best chance of the match, Gardner's mazy dribble in which he beat three Rovers defenders, gave the Burnley forward another chance and this time, he beat Fairbrother with a first-time shot.

Burnley
E. Adams; J. Marshall; H. Mather; T. Gardner; A. Woodruff; J. Lomax; N. Dougall; C. Cooke; G. Knight; R. Brocklebank; R. Hornby

Blackburn Rovers
J. Fairbrother; E. Lancely; W. Crook; F. Chivers; R. Pryde; J. Wightman; J. Weddle; R. Cahill; T. Hargreaves; J. Brindle; D. Stanfield

Attendance: 3,731

Match 73
9 November 1940
Blackburn Rovers 1 Burnley 1

When play began, Rovers only had ten men, Len Butt being late. Burnley took advantage of this, almost taking the lead with their first attack of the game. Gardner fed Dougall but as he prepared to shoot, he was well tackled by Walter Crook, who was injured in the process.

Blackburn's first attack also almost brought about a goal with Fairbrother saving at the feet of Guest, who had rounded both Marshall and Mather. At the other end, Brocklebank shot wide before Gardner's header from a Knight cross brought a good save out of Owen.

Following his late arrival, Butt was soon in the thick of the action and headed narrowly wide following good work by Hargreaves. Though the game was played at a fast pace, the first half was goalless.

Good work by Knight and Gardner led to an opening for Hornby but he shot well wide when in a good position. Rovers took the lead in the 71st minute when CHIVERS took a free-kick some 25 yards out. As the shot curled into the goalmouth, Butt tried to head it, his action completely deceiving Fairbrother, who was rooted to the spot. Burnley were unaffected by the reverse and after several businesslike assaults on the Rovers goal, they equalised ten minutes from time when GARDNER beat Owen with a shot which entered the net via the post.

Brocklebank did force the ball over the line in the closing moments, though he was adjudged offside.

Blackburn Rovers
C. Owen; E. Lancely; W. Crook; D. Anderson; R. Pryde; F. Chivers; W. Rogers; L. Butt; T. Hargreaves; P. Dickie; W. Guest

Burnley
J. Fairbrother; A. Marshall; H. Mather; J. Loughran; A. Woodruff; J. Lomax; N. Dougall; T. Gardner; R. Brocklebank; G. Knight; R. Hornby

Attendance: 1,100

Match 74
1 February 1941
Burnley 2 Blackburn Rovers 1

Rovers should have gone ahead after two minutes when a move started by Butt ended with Dickie completely missing his kick with the goal at his mercy. The visitors again had a chance to open the scoring on five minutes but Conway saved well from Guest.

Yet it was Burnley who took the lead in the seventh minute when Kippax's turn of speed left Pryde in his wake and as Roxburgh came out to narrow the angle, he slipped the ball inside for KNIGHT to put the Clarets 1-0 up. Three minutes later another quick raid enabled Burnley to increase their lead. Kippax again made the goal, stepping inside both Pryde and Lanceley before feeding BRIGHT who shot hard past Roxburgh into the corner of the net. Brocklebank almost added a third on the half-hour mark but his free-kick, awarded for a foul on Knight, crashed against the foot of Roxburgh's left-hand post.

Blackburn reduced the arrears five minutes after the interval through ROGERS. The goal came as a result of a long kick upfield by Roxburgh, Butt gaining possession before passing to the Rovers winger to shoot home.

Gardner almost extended the Clarets lead but his well struck shot was scrambled round the post by Roxburgh. Kippax should have scored a third for Burnley when put clean through but crashed the ball against the Blackburn 'keeper's legs. Gardner gave Kippax another chance in the closing minutes of the game but the Burnley centre-forward was brought down by Pryde who received a severe telling-off from the referee.

Burnley
H. Conway; R. Johnson; H. Mather; T. Gardner; A. Woodruff; J. Loughran; R. Hornby; R. Brocklebank; F. Kippax; G. Knight; R. Bright

Blackburn Rovers
A. Roxburgh; E. Lanceley; D. Anderson; J. Wightman; R. Pryde; F. Chivers; W. Rogers; L. Butt; R. Shankley; P. Dickie; W. Guest

Attendance: 2,310

Match 75
15 March 1941
Blackburn Rovers 3 Burnley 2

The first half was not very entertaining, the standard of football and the keen rivalry which usually characterises the meeting of these old foes was rarely visible.

In the early stages of the game, Burnley's forwards frequently fell into obvious offside traps and it was Rovers inside-forward Len BUTT who opened the scoring after 12 minutes, beating Holdcroft with a low drive from the edge of the area. Though the home side had most of the play in the first half, the Clarets equalised in the 44th minute when KNIGHT shot high into the net from fully 20 yards. Rovers 'keeper Roxburgh, who was 'guesting' from Blackpool had no chance.

Blackburn regained the lead midway through the second half through CARTER but in the 76th minute, KNIGHT scored his and Burnley's second goal to level things up. The game looked to be heading for a draw but in the closing stages, the Rovers were awarded a rather dubious penalty and BUTT stepped up to send Holdcroft the wrong way.

Blackburn Rovers
A. Roxburgh; M. Reeday; D. Anderson; G. Farrow; R. Pryde; F. Chivers; J. Chew; L. Butt; G. Cross; K. Carter; T. Pearson

Burnley
H. Holdcroft; L. Snowden; H. Mather; T. Gardner; A. Woodruff; A. Robinson; R. Bright; R. Brocklebank; F. Kippax; G. Knight; R. Hornby

Attendance: 2,000

Match 76
22 November 1941
Blackburn Rovers 3 Burnley 2

With Rovers a man short at the outset, Burnley soon came into the picture and after good work by Woodruff, Brocklebank brought a fine save out of Conway. Yet it was Rovers who took the lead in the 16th minute when Rogers made progress down the middle before passing inside for GLAISTER to score past Holdcroft.

Soon afterwards, Rovers were at full strength and they celebrated the arrival of Bryson with a series of raids on the Burnley goal. Maudsley brought a good save out of Holdcroft before Pearson had the ball taken off his toes as he shaped to shoot.

Early in the second half, Burnley should have drawn level but Kippax shot straight at Conway. Ten minutes into the second period and Rovers increased their lead. From a pass by Bryson, Rogers sent the ball hard against the Burnley bar and as it came down, MAUDSLEY smashed it into the net. Two minutes later, Salmon crossed for KIPPAX to pull a goal back and though Burnley went close to equalising on a number of occasions, they had to wait until the 82nd minute before drawing level. After good work by Gardner, KIPPAX was left with the simple task of side-footing home from close range for his and Burnley's second goal.

Both sides went all out for the winner but it was latecomer BRYSON who scored with a snap shot to give Rovers victory.

Blackburn Rovers
H. Conway; G. Forbes; W. Taylor; P. Chivers; R. Pryde; G. Glaister; R. Maudsley; D. Dickie; W. Rogers; W. Bryson; T. Pearson

Burnley
H. Holdcroft; R. Johnson; P. Kirkman; M. Salmon; A. Woodruff; A. Robinson; T. Gardner; R. Brocklebank; F. Kippax; G. Knight; H. Whalley

Attendance: 1,500

Match 77
29 November 1941
Burnley 0 Blackburn Rovers 0

Both sides took time to get to grips with the muddy conditions after the usually so reliable Bob Pryde miskicked in the first few minutes of the game to give Kippax an opening. The Clarets centre-forward's shot took a deflection off Taylor before Conway smothered the ball.

The home side was on top for much of the first half and Gardner, who was the pick of the Burnley forwards, shot into the side-netting with Conway beaten.

The players turned round immediately at the interval due to the fast fading light. Kippax missed a great chance when Gardner gave him the ball with only the 'keeper to beat and then Conway kept out a fierce drive by Whalley. Pryde was prominent at the heart of the Rovers defence and it was from one of his clearances that the visitors almost took the lead. Rogers fastened on to the centre-half's hefty punt upfield and raced clear of the Burnley defence before shooting narrowly wide.

In the closing stages, play became very scrappy though Brocklebank put in a shot, which went just over the bar.

Burnley
H. Holdcroft; R. Johnson; P. Kirkman; M. Salmon; A. Woodruff; A. Robinson; T. Gardner; R. Brocklebank; F. Kippax; R. Hornby; H. Whalley

Blackburn Rovers
H. Conway; G. Forbes; W. Taylor; A. Whiteside; R. Pryde; F. Chivers; R. Maudsley; G. Glaister; W. Rogers; E. Wilde; T. Pearson

Attendance: 3,895

Match 78
14 March 1942
Blackburn Rovers 6 Burnley 2

This was a remarkable performance by a Blackburn Rovers side that lost two players before the interval and played the whole of the second half with nine men!

The Clarets had the better of the opening exchanges with Gardner sending a shot against the legs of Conway but within seven minutes, RILET, receiving the ball from Butt, cut through the Burnley defence before shooting past Sagar. Two minutes later, PEARSON extended the home side's lead . With just quarter-of-an-hour gone, PEARSON cut inside Ward to score his second goal and put Rovers 3-0 up.

Rovers left-back Taylor was injured in a Burnley raid and though he spent a short time on the wing, he was eventually forced to leave the action. Rilet was the other Blackburn player forced to quit the game following a hefty challenge from Burnley's 'guest' 'keeper Ted Sagar. BROCKLEBANK reduced the arrears with a header from Hornby's centre as Burnley ended the first half in the ascendancy.

Though Rovers only had nine men, they were playing with great spirit and in the 55th minute, BUTT put them 4-1 up following a corner. Ten minutes from the end, BUTT scored another and after BROCKLEBANK had again reduced the arrears by heading home his second goal of the game from another Hornby corner, DAWSON scored Rovers sixth goal with the last kick of the game.

Blackburn Rovers
H. Conway; G. Forbes; W. Taylor; A. Whiteside; R. Pryde; F. Chivers; J. Dawson; L. Butt; E. Rilet; G. Glaister; T. Pearson

Burnley
T. Sagar; A. Ward; L. Snowden; J. Readett; A. Woodruff; J. Lomax; T. Gardner; S. Deverall; R. Brocklebank; R. Gibson; R. Hornby

Attendance: 3,534

Match 79
28 March 1942
Burnley 2 Blackburn Rovers 0

As a spectacle, the game had not much to offer because for a long time, the defences were on top. Burnley had to win by five clear goals to pass into the next round of the Lancashire Cup. Though their victory was not by the required margin, it was a fine performance by a side lacking many of its regular players.

After a goalless first half in which both 'keepers had little to do, the Clarets took the lead in the 64th minute when Gardner centred to JACK-SON who headed past Barron. Rovers appealed for offside but the referee had no hesitation in awarding the goal.

The home side was greatly encouraged by this goal but it was not until two minutes from time that they added to their one-goal lead.

Jackson, eluding Pryde's challenge, sent a shot against the angle of the goal and BROCKLEBANK following up, scored from the rebound.

Burnley
J. Strong; R. Johnson; L. Snowden; S. Crossland; A. Woodruff; G. Bray; T. Gardner; R. Brocklebank; H. Jackson; R. Waddington; J. Bright

Blackburn Rovers
J. Barron; G. Forbes; R. Ancell; A. Whiteside; R. Pryde; F. Chivers; H. McShane; L. Butt; E. Rilet; G. Glaister; T. Pearson

Attendance: 3,153

Match 80
29 August 1942
Blackburn Rovers 3 Burnley 3

In a game which produced a first half full of thrills and a pace which both sides found impossible to maintain after the interval, the Clarets can consider themselves unlucky not to have won the game.

Certainly, they were unfortunate not to have been 2-0 up in the opening minutes as what appeared to be good goals by Bright and O'Donnell were disallowed for offside.

Rovers, who were reinforced by several Preston North End players took the lead on the half-hour when ANCELL beat Robinson to the ball before firing past Holdcroft. Minutes later, DOUGAL extended the home side's lead with a downward header following good work by Pearson.

Hugh O'DONNELL pulled a goal back for the visitors just before half-time, side-footing home from close range after fine approach play by Hornby.

Early in the second half, the Clarets equalised when BRIGHT cut inside Taylor and fired home an unstoppable shot past John in the Rovers goal. Rovers lead was restored in the 78th minute when McLAREN headed home Aspden's pin-point cross. Time was running out when Burnley centre-forward Bob BROCKLEBANK levelled the scores, converting Gardner's centre from the right. Rovers thought they had snatched victory right at the death but Dougal was penalised for a foul on Holdcroft.

Blackburn Rovers
W. John; W. Taylor; D. Anderson; A. Whiteside; R. Pryde; W. Robertson; T. Aspden; A. McLaren; J. Dougal; R. Ancell; T. Pearson

Burnley
H. Holdcroft; L. Snowden; P. Kirkman; A. Robinson; A. Woodruff; J. Lomax; T. Gardner; R. Brocklebank; H. O'Donnell; R. Hornby; J. Bright

Attendance: 2,000

Match 81
5 September 1942
Burnley 1 Blackburn Rovers 0

Though the first half was somewhat scrappy with the defences on top throughout, Burnley held a definite territorial advantage. In fact, Rovers' only chance in the first half fell to McLaren whose powerful shot was turned round the post by Holdcroft.

Rovers increased the pressure after the interval and three free-kicks in quick succession just outside the Burnley penalty area was evidence of desperate defending tactics by the home side. From one of these, Woodruff headed round the post with Holdcroft beaten.

At the other end, a fine run by Gardner resulted in the Clarets winger being fouled by Ancell. From the free-kick, Lomax's well-struck drive was pushed over the bar by John. The corner was hit deep into the Rovers' penalty area where TAYLOR under pressure from O'Donnell, turned the ball into his own net. This inspired the Clarets and both O'Donnell and Jackson went close before Brocklebank tore a muscle and hobbled off to leave Burnley with ten men.

The remainder of the match was played in the Burnley half but despite virtual constant pressure by Rovers, the Clarets defence held out to claim a memorable victory.

Burnley
H. Holdcroft; L. Snowden; P. Kirkman; A. Robinson; A. Woodruff; J. Lomax; T. Gardner; R. Brocklebank; H. O'Donnell; S. Jackson; J. Bright

Blackburn Rovers
W. John; W. Taylor; D. Anderson; A. Whiteside; R. Pryde; R. Ancell; T. Aspden; A. McLaren; J. Dougal; G. Glaister; T. Pearson

Attendance: 1,972

Match 82
26 December 1942
Blackburn Rovers 3 Burnley 1

Rovers dominated this Boxing Day clash and Holdcroft in the Burnley goal was called into action on a number of occasions in the opening quarter of the game. The home side opened the scoring after twenty minutes when PEARSON headed home a corner from the right. Holdcroft got both hands to the ball but it was greasy and slipped from his grasp and over the line before he could recover.

GARDNER then equalised for the visitors in what was the Clarets' first real attack. Jackson made ground on the left but had to delay his centre because the inside-forwards weren't ready to receive it. Ultimately, it was Gardner who arrived first to head home the centre-forward's cross.

Midway through the second half, Wigglesworth, the young Burnley centre-half hesitated between passing back to Holdcroft and putting into touch. This allowed LUCAS the opportunity to take the ball of his toes and shoot into the net from close range.

PEARSON, who was a big factor in Rovers' success, made the issue certain when, after beating three defenders, he fired home from 25 yards out. The Rovers forward had a late opportunity to complete his hat-trick but Holdcroft made an excellent save.

Blackburn Rovers
H. Conway; G. Forbes; D. Anderson; A. Whiteside; R. Pryde; F. Hindle; G. James; H. Stephan; J. Melia; W. Lucas; T. Pearson

Burnley
H. Holdcroft; A. Robinson; L. Snowden; H. Rudman; H. Wigglesworth; C. Webster; T. Gardner; R. Waddington; S. Jackson; R. Hornby; H. O'Donnell

Attendance: 8,413

Match 83
2 January 1943
Burnley 0 Blackburn Rovers 0

Whilst it was a game in which the honours went to the defences, it has to be said that the Clarets would have won easily if it hadn't been for an inspired display by Conway in the Rovers goal.

He proved equal to all Burnley could throw at him and in the 23rd minute, saved O'Donnell's penalty-kick after Waddington had been fouled in the area by Forbes. The Rovers 'keeper leapt to his right and turned the ball over the bar. This was followed by more equally excellent saves, especially in the closing stages of the first half.

Early in the second half, Rovers centre-forward Dougal got clean through but with only Holdcroft to beat, he didn't even force him to move, shooting straight into the Keeper's hands. It wasn't long before Burnley were back on the attack and Conway had to turn over Rudman's 35-yard shot. A minute later he made an even better save from Kippax, turning his shot from point-blank range round the post. The Rovers 'keeper later parried a Rudman shot onto his own crossbar and though Gardner forced the ball over the line, he was given offside.

Bob Pryde was a tower of strength at the heart of the Blackburn defence and his untiring resistance was as much a factor as Conway's brilliant keeping in ensuring that Rovers kept a clean sheet.

Burnley
H. Holdcroft; L. Snowden; D. Watson; H. Rudman; A. Woodruff;
C. Webster; T. Gardner; R. Brocklebank; H. O'Donnell; R. Waddington;
F. Kippax

Blackburn Rovers
H. Conway; G. Forbes; D. Anderson; A. Whiteside; R. Pryde;
W. Robertson; J. Melia; G. James; J. Dougal; D. Entwistle; L. Cook

Attendance: 2,640

Match 84
19 February 1944
Burnley 5 Blackburn Rovers 1

Placed in the running for qualification in the League Cup by their double victory over Blackpool, Burnley were in a very determined mood against Blackburn Rovers and took the lead as early as the seventh minute when

Bob Pryde failed to clear and let in BROCKLEBANK whose first-time shot gave Conway no chance.

Rovers had in fact started the game with ten men but shortly after the Clarets' opening goal, were brought to full strength by the appearance of Whiteside.

However, Burnley continued to dominate, and BROCKLEBANK netted his and the Clarets' second goal after 14 minutes as Geddes lobbed the ball into the Rovers goalmouth. BROCKLEBANK, the Burnley centre-forward completed his hat-trick shortly before half-time when his 30-yard shot beat the despairing dive of Conway in the Rovers goal, although he appeared to get his finger tips to the ball.

Six minutes after the interval, WATSON scored from Brocklebank's pass and then in the 65th minute, BROCKLEBANK netted Burnley's fifth goal with a swerving shot which completely deceived Conway.

At the other end, Strong saved well from Guest before ASPDEN netted a consolation goal for the visitors, cutting in from the left-wing and firing high into the roof of the net from the edge of the area.

Burnley
J. Strong; D. Geddes; H. Mather; H. Rudman; A. Woodruff; C. Webster; T. Gardner; F. Reid; R. Brocklebank; D. Watson; H. Sargent

Blackburn Rovers
H. Conway; W. Taylor; W. Crook; A. Whiteside; R. Pryde; W. Robertson; T. Aspden; J. Wharton; J. Dougal; H. Stephan; W. Guest

Attendance: 7,107

Match 85
26 February 1944
Blackburn Rovers 2 Burnley 0

Burnley made several early raids on the Rovers goal but because they neglected to exploit the first-time pass, their efforts to break through the home side's defence were easily checked. The Clarets centre-forward Harry Potts often found himself offside as both Brocklebank and Gardner delayed their passes.

It was Rovers who went ahead after 35 minutes when Mather missed his tackle on McSHANE, allowing the winger the opportunity to get in a shot that gave Strong no chance.

Midway through the second period, Burnley had a good chance to equalise when Gardner beat several defenders but instead of crossing the ball into the middle where his team-mates were waiting, he was caught in two minds, allowing Crook to nip in and put the ball out for a corner.

Rovers extended their lead in the closing stages of the game when GUEST rounded Woodruff before shooting past the advancing Strong in the Burnley goal.

Blackburn Rovers
H. Conway; W. Taylor; W. Crook; A. Whiteside; R. Pryde; W. Robertson; H. McShane; J. Bibby; J. Dougal; H. Stephan; W. Guest

Burnley
J. Strong; D. Watson; H. Mather; H. Rudman; A. Woodruff; C. Webster; T. Gardner; H. Potts; R. Brocklebank; J. Reid; H. Sargent

Attendance: 5,000

Match 86
18 March 1944
Blackburn Rovers 2 Burnley 1

Burnley had to recruit a player from the crowd for their Lancashire Cup-tie game with the Rovers for, of the fifteen players listed as probables, five of them were unable to make the journey! A board was sent round the ground with the inscription, 'Wanted a player, forward preferred,' and Private Edwardson of the Royal Army Service Corps offered his services.

Blackburn made most of the early running and went ahead after 11 minutes, a shot by STEPHAN going into the net off a Burnley defender. Five minutes later, Edwardson got away on the left to provide BURNS with an easy chance of equalising. The goal seemed to spur the Clarets on and both Reid and Brocklebank came close to giving them the lead.

The second half was a little disappointing. Scoring chances were few and far between and it seemed that neither side was going to break the deadlock. Only four minutes remained when ROGERS headed Rovers in front following an accurate cross by Dougal.

Blackburn Rovers
H. Conway; G. Forbes; W. Crook; A. Whiteside; R. Pryde; W. Robertson; W. Rogers; H. Stephan; F. Coates; D. Marshall; J. Dougal

Burnley
R. Walmsley; A. Robinson; D. Watson; H. Rudman; A. Woodruff; C. Webster; T. Gardner; M. Burns; R. Brocklebank; J. Reid; J. Edwardson

Attendance: 3,000

Match 87
25 March 1944
Burnley 2 Blackburn Rovers 2

After promising Burnley raids had been thwarted by offside tactics, Rovers took up the running and STEPHAN opened the scoring for the visitors. The Rovers inside-right was left completely unmarked at the far post as Barton's cross found its way through a crowd of players, leaving him the simple task of side-footing into an empty net.

In the 25th minute, Rovers went 2-0 up when ROGERS cut inside Scott before beating Bentley in the Burnley goal with a fast, rising shot. Ten minutes later, GARDNER, playing at inside-right, scored with a well-placed shot from Holden's centre. There were still eight minutes of the first half remaining when GARDNER scored his and Burnley's second goal. Receiving the ball from Brocklebank, he moved into the Rovers' penalty area before beating Conway from ten yards out.

The second half was a disappointing affair with Rovers having little difficulty in maintaining a defensive role. As a result, there was no further scoring, although Anderson nearly snatched victory for the visitors with a long-range shot that beat Bentley before striking an upright!

Burnley
G. Bentley; J. Readay; P. Scott; H. Rudman; A. Woodruff; C. Webster; T. Smith; T. Gardner; R. Brocklebank; J. Reid; K. Holden

Blackburn Rovers
H. Conway; G. Forbes; W. Crook; A. Whiteside; R. Pryde; C. Woods; W. Rogers; H. Stephan; T. Wyles; D. Anderson; J. Barton

Attendance: 4,769

Match 88
26 August 1944
Burnley 1 Blackburn Rovers 1

In a dull first half, the first real chance for either side came Burnley's way in the 20th minute when Patterson went through but his shot struck Conway and was cleared. At the other end, Graham tested Strong with a hard close-range shot and then Stephan tried his luck with a powerful header, just missing the target by inches.

Early in the second half, Burnley's Reid shot wide when well placed.

Strong had just saved well from Bibby but then was beaten in the 57th minute as GRAHAM gave Rovers the lead following good work by Cook.

The home side then gradually began to get on top and dominated the latter stages of the game. There were only three minutes left when Gardner broke away and his brilliant run ended with the Clarets' equalising goal. REID provided the finishing touch to the movement but it looked as if Gardner's shot would have found the net without any assistance.

Burnley

J. Strong; F. Gallimore; J. Marshall; L. Martindale; A. Woodruff; C. Webster; T. Gardner; J. Reid; R. Brocklebank; M. Patterson; J. Kinghorn

Blackburn Rovers

H. Conway; G. Forbes; W. Crook; A. Whiteside; R. Pryde; D. Anderson; J. Bibby; H. Brian; J. Graham; H. Stephan; L. Cook

Attendance: 5,945

Match 89
2 September 1944
Blackburn Rovers 0 Burnley 2

The game opened briskly and both sides had chances to open the scoring. Brocklebank brought a fine save out of Conway while at the other end, Graham's chip was well held under his crossbar by Strong. Burnley took the lead when Harry POTTS shot hard and low past Conway, the ball entering the net off the inside of the 'keeper's left-hand post.

Aided by a stiff breeze, Burnley kept Rovers on the defensive but failed to press home the advantage. Conway continued to have a busy time while Strong was for a long spell, a spectator. After a centre from Cook had gone begging, Kinghorn headed just over from Potts' pass. In the closing moments of the first half, Rovers almost equalised when Bibby struck the foot of the post with a first-time shot.

With the wind in their favour, Rovers had more of the play in the second half. Cook missed an easy chance before hitting the bar with a powerful 20-yard drive that had Strong beaten.

Four minutes from the end, Potts broke through the Blackburn defence before squaring the ball for KINGHORN to put Burnley further ahead.

Blackburn Rovers
H. Conway; G. Forbes; W. Crook; A. Whiteside; F. Hindle; J. Wightman;
H. Smith; J. Bibby; J. Graham; H. Stephan; L. Cook

Burnley
J. Strong; F. Gallimore; H. Mather; L. Martindale; A. Woodruff; C. Webster;
T. Gardner; H. Potts; R. Brocklebank; M. Patterson; J. Kinghorn

Attendance: 2,000

Match 90
25 December 1944
Blackburn Rovers 2 Burnley 4

Burnley's Christmas Day superiority over the Rovers in the first match of
the FA League Cup qualifying round was even more pronounced than
the score would indicate.

The Clarets were not long in getting on top and Gardner and Kippax
were soon on the move. The forwards looked like scoring more than once
but Conway in the Rovers' goal produced some memorable saves and the
interval arrived with the game still goalless.

The second half was only two minutes old when Burnley broke the
deadlock. Following a brilliant piece of play by the Clarets two wingers,
GARDNER worked his way close in to beat Conway all ends up.
Burnley's second goal came in the 59th minute and was the result of a
movement in which all the forwards took part, Gardner finishing by
placing the ball at the feet of Bob BROCKLEBANK for him to crash the
ball into the net.

BROCKLEBANK added a third ten minutes later, converting a pass
from Kippax after the winger had beaten several opponents.

Rovers pulled a goal back through COATES, who was left completely
unmarked at Langton's corner. With just twenty minutes to play,
KIPPAX capped a great run in which he beat three Rovers players before
shooting past Conway. STEPHAN reduced the arrears for Rovers but the
home side's spirited response was too late in coming.

Blackburn Rovers
H. Conway; W. Taylor; W. Crook; A. Whiteside; G. Forbes; F. Egerton;
H. Smith; W. Fairweather; F. Coates; H. Stephan; R. Langton

Burnley
J. Strong; F. Gallimore; H. Mather; C. Webster; A. Woodruff; G. Bray;
T. Gardner; L. Martindale; R. Brocklebank; J. Bright; F. Kippax

Attendance: 9,730

Match 91
30 December 1944
Burnley 4 Blackburn Rovers 1

The opening minutes of this game were enough to demonstrate that Burnley were the better team. Sustained pressure by the Clarets straight from the kick-off brought a goal after only eight minutes when DRYDEN shot through a cluster of players from close range. Kippax then hit the underside of the bar but Forbes cleared the danger before any Burnley forward could capitalise on the rebound.

Blackburn equalised against the run of play in the 22nd minute when STRONG in the Burnley goal in trying to fist away a high cross from Smith, deflected the ball into his own net.

The second half was a one-sided affair as the Clarets attacked from start to finish. DRYDEN scored his and Burnley's second goal in the 52nd minute before BROCKLEBANK headed powerfully past Conway for the Clarets' third goal on the hour mark. GARDNER then capped a fine solo effort by netting the fourth in the 86th minute. In the closing minutes, Blackburn's goal was bombarded from all angles but managed to hold out.

Burnley
J. Strong; F. Gallimore; A. Robinson; L. Martindale; A. Woodruff; K. Holden; T. Gardner; M. Burns; R. Brocklebank; J. Dryden; F. Kippax

Blackburn Rovers
H. Conway; G. Forbes; W. Taylor; A. Whiteside; F. Hindle; F. Egerton; H. Smith; J. Bibby; F. Coates; L. Cook; H. Rudman
Attendance: 8,948

Match 92
9 May 1945
Burnley 3 Blackburn Rovers 1

Neither side was anything like full strength and Rovers had to call on Bradford, the Clarets reserve centre-half to play for them!

Whittaker of Brentford, the son of a former Burnley player took Woodruff's place in the Clarets side whilst Rudman lined up at outside-left.

MARTINDALE opened the scoring for the home side after 29 minutes, heading through from a corner by Gardner. Four minutes later, RUDMAN with a fine first-time drive from over 30 yards out added a second and then in the last minute of the first half, MARTINDALE's shot was helped into the net by Rovers young 'keeper Tattersall.

It wasn't until the last few minutes of the game that Blackburn showed any signs of reducing the arrears and when they did so in the 85th minute through Jack SMITH, he looked distinctly offside!

Burnley
B. Tonge; F. Gallimore; A. Robinson; C. Webster; A. Whittaker; G. Bray; T. Gardner; L. Martindale; R. Brocklebank; J. Drury; H. Rudman

Blackburn Rovers
S. Tattersall; W. Forbes; W. Crook; F. Egerton; J. Bradford; E. Bell; J. Smith; J. Bibby; F. Coates; L. Cook; H. Smith

Attendance: 2,308

Match 93
20 October 1945
Blackburn Rovers 4 Burnley 2

Rovers took the lead midway through the first half with a most controversial goal. Both Wyles and Stephan seemed to be in offside positions and indeed, hesitated, waiting for the referee's whistle. The Burnley defenders, too, waited for the whistle until it was too late. Strong parried Wyles' shot but the supporting STEPHAN slammed the rebound into the roof of the net. Woodruff, who was the nearest defender, protested strongly to both linesman and referee but was overruled.

Burnley equalised early in the second half through HAYS, following good work by Loughran. , Rovers went ahead through a penalty for a foul on WYLES, who took the kick himself. The home side extended their lead when HALL came inside Mulvaney before hitting the ball hard into the corner of the net as he was being tackled. HAYS reduced the arrears, netting his and the Clarets' second goal with a dropping cross shot into the far corner. STEPHAN made it 4-2 to Rovers with a downward header from Campbell's cross and though Hold got the ball into the net for the visitors, he was given offside.

Towards the end of the game, Hold's shot beat Barron's despairing dive and hit the underside of the crossbar before bouncing down on the goal-line.

Blackburn Rovers
J. Barron; G. Forbes; W. Crook; F. Egerton; F. Hindle; E. Bell; W. Hall; W. Rogers; C. Wyles; H. Stephan; J. Campbell

Burnley
J. Strong; D. Mulvaney; H. Mather; H. Spencer; A. Woodruff; J. Loughran; T. Gardner; D. Meek; O. Hold; H. Rudman; J. Hays

Attendance: 8,228

Match 94
27 October 1945
Burnley 1 Blackburn Rovers 4

It was a day of triumph for Cecil Wyles, the Rovers ex-Everton centre-forward who celebrated his mid-week signing with four goals.

Nevertheless, it was Burnley who took the lead in the 13th minute when HOLD shook off two defenders and scored with a hard, low drive into the right-hand corner of Barron's goal. The Clarets were well on top for the first half-an-hour and Barron saved well from both Hold and Hays. The home side were unlucky not to be awarded a penalty when Kippax had his legs taken from under him as he cut inside to shoot, well inside the area.

Blackburn equalised against the run of play when they were awarded a penalty following a handball offence. WYLES sent Breedon the wrong way to send the sides in level at the interval. Early in the second half, Mather miskicked a clearance straight to Hall who beat the full-back before centring for WYLES to score his and Rovers' second goal. Minutes later, the Rovers centre-forward netted his hat-trick when heading home Campbell's corner.

Burnley came close to reducing the arrears on a couple of occasions with Hold beating three men before forcing Barron into making a good save at the foot of the post and Hays shooting narrowly wide from a difficult angle.

WYLES' fourth goal was a magnificent drive from fully 30 yards and Breedon the Burnley 'keeper injured himself in trying to save it!

Burnley
J. Breedon; D. Mulvaney; H. Mather; T. Wilson; A. Woodruff; H. Rudman; J. Hays; T. Gardner; O. Hold; D. Meek; F. Kippax

Blackburn Rovers
J. Barron; W. Crook; A. Green; G. Glaister; G. Forbes; E. Bell; W. Hall; W. Rogers; C. Wyles; H. Stephan; J. Campbell

Attendance: 7,964

Match 95
18 October 1947
Blackburn Rovers 1 Burnley 2

The Clarets took the lead in the second minute in the most unusual fashion. TOMLINSON the Rovers right-back found himself harassed by

Hays, who was trying to take advantage of a right-wing centre and in panic, he hooked the ball back to Marks, who was starting to come out. The pass went over his head into the net!

The goal acted as a spur to the home side and their forwards piled on the pressure as they went in search of an equaliser. The Burnley goal had several narrow escapes with both Bray and Brown heading away point-blank shots and Strong being called upon to punch clear some dangerous crosses from Langton.

Within minutes of the restart, Burnley scored a second goal when MORRIS with a typical burst of speed, raced clear of the Rovers defence after Higgins had been caught in two minds and then placed the ball wide of Marks, as the 'keeper tried to narrow the angles.

An attempt by Potts to hook a Marks clearance out to Hays on the volley, resulted in the ball landing at the feet of Oakes who raced away before crossing to VENTERS who made no mistake from close in. Chew and then Billington scraped the Rovers crossbar with first-time efforts but the Clarets centre-forward missed badly after being put clear by Morris when he only had Marks to beat.

In the dying moments of the game, Pryde and Potts were involved in an incident that left the Burnley player writhing on the ground in agony. Both players were given a stern lecture by the referee but were lucky to stay on the field!

Blackburn Rovers
G. Marks; R. Tomlinson; G. Higgins; T. Baldwin; R. Pryde; E. Bell; J. Oakes; L. Graham; V. Godwin; A. Venters; R. Langton

Burnley
J. Strong; A. Woodruff; H. Mather; R. Attwell; A. Brown; G. Bray; J. Chew; W. Morris; J. Billingham; H. Potts; J. Hays

Attendance: 41,635

Match 96
6 March 1948
Burnley 0 Blackburn Rovers 0

Prior to this East Lancashire Derby, Burnley hadn't scored a League goal since they won at Middlesbrough at the end of January and if their display in this game is anything to go by, it could be another twelve months before they find the back of the net!

The Clarets forward line was unenterprising and slow-moving and caused very few problems for the Rovers' defence.

As a Derby game, it provided the crowd with few thrills but much hard play and a struggle in which defences were on top. Goals were missed by both sides and Potts had probably the easiest chance of the first half when he collected the ball on the edge of the Rovers' box, turned Baldwin but then shot yards wide with Hayhurst out of his goal. Graham had a similar chance at the start of the second half and though it still didn't result in a goal, he forced Strong into making a save.

Towards the end of this rather lamentable exhibition of football, there were strong claims for a penalty when Rovers centre-half, Bob Pryde appeared to stop the ball with his forearm inside the penalty area. The referee, who it has to be said wasn't up with play, overruled the infringement and Rovers came away from Turf Moor with a valuable point.

Burnley
J. Strong; J. Loughran; H. Mather; R. Attwell; A. Brown; G. Bray; J. Hays; J. Knight; J. Billingham; H. Potts; J. Chew

Blackburn Rovers
S. Hayhurst; G. Higgins; E. Bell; J. Baldwin; R. Pryde; H. Morton; J. Campbell; E. Crossan; L. Graham; E. Murphy; R. Langton

Attendance: 44,240

Match 97
8 March 1952
Blackburn Rovers 3 Burnley 1

After a rather nervous opening quarter-of-an-hour of this FA Cup sixth round tie, both sides settled down to play some attractive football, though it has to be said that the Clarets looked the most dangerous.

Burnley took the lead after 38 minutes when Billy Elliott was brought down by Suart. Whilst the Clarets winger was receiving treatment off the pitch, Adamson took the free-kick and as the ball ran loose, Shannon crossed for CHEW to hit home. Elliott resumed, obviously shaken but five minutes later, he was laid out for a second time in the game and switched wings with Holden.

Rovers equalised in first half injury time when following three corners in quick succession, Glover squared the ball for NIGHTINGALE to beat Strong.

Burnley were still on top in the second half when in the 57th minute,

Rovers went 2-1 up after a rare foray into the Clarets' half. Nightingale, the scorer of Rovers' first goal, made progress down the left-wing before crossing for HOLMES to head powerfully past Strong. Event then, the Clarets fans could be forgiven for thinking their team would soon equalise as the visitors had dominated the game.

Yet with just eight minutes remaining, it was Rovers who scored the game's next goal. Eckersley turned defence into attack with a clearance that found Holmes. The Blackburn centre-forward beat Jock Aird and then rounded Tommy Cummings before pulling the ball back to the unmarked GLOVER to slot home.

In the time that remained, Strong made a great save from Crossan while at the other end, Holden hit the crossbar for the second successive game!

Blackburn Rovers
R. Elvy; R. Suart; W. Eckersley; J. Campbell; W. Kelly; R. Clayton; J. Wharton; E. Crossan; W. Holmes; A. Nightingale; A. Glover

Burnley
J. Strong; J. Aird; H. Mather; J. Adamson; T. Cumming; R. Attwell; J. Chew; W. Morris; W. Holden; L. Shannon; W. Elliott

Attendance: 52,920

Match 98
18 October 1958
Burnley 0 Blackburn Rovers 0

Blackburn Rovers had most of the play in the first half when Colin McDonald in the Burnley goal thrilled the crowd with some breathtaking saves from full-blooded shots from Dobing, Stephenson and MacLeod.

Burnley's best period in the first half came with just five minutes to play before the interval when Jimmy McIlroy, the Clarets Northern Ireland international inside-forward crashed a shot at Leyland in the Blackburn goal, which he did well to turn over the bar. Also in this period, Robson, Pointer and Pilkington all had attempts blocked without being able to find a way through.

There had been a little light relief midway through the first half when Burnley centre-half Tommy Cummings suffered the indignity of having his shorts give way under strain and stress and finished by wearing two pairs!

Towards the end of the game, Rovers made a last desperate attempt to snatch a winner but their shooting had more power than direction and one effort from Stephenson almost cleared the covered end!

It was mostly a midfield struggle, dour and remorseless with the finer arts of the game smothered by the determination of the tackling.

Burnley
C. McDonald; J. Angus; D. Smith; R. Seith; T. Cummings; J. Adamson; D. Newlands; J. McIlroy; R. Pointer; J. Robson; B. Pilkington

Blackburn Rovers
H. Leyland; K. Taylor; W. Eckersley; R. Clayton; M. Woods; M. McGrath; B. Douglas; P. Dobing; T. Johnson; R. Stephenson; A. MacLeod

Attendance: 41,961

Match 99
28 January 1959
Blackburn Rovers 1 Burnley 2

The first meeting of these two clubs in the fourth round of the FA Cup had been abandoned but was brought to a conclusion at the second attempt four days later. The pitch was still reputed to be icebound but a heavy coating of sand tended to disguise its faults and deficiencies!

In the abandoned game, Rovers swept into attack with the obvious determination to snatch an early goal and they repeated the plan in this game. Rovers' ambitions were realised in the 10th minute when Clayton pushed through a pass to the right, Johnson combined with DOBING who smashed the ball past a startled McDonald in the Burnley goal. Rovers had completely dominated the first half yet the Clarets almost equalised in the 44th minute when Jimmy Robson hit the crossbar and from the rebound, Pilkington sliced the ball wide.

In the opening stages of the second half, both Leyland and McDonald were called into action on a number of occasions as the game swung from end to end. Vernon thought he had put Rovers 2-0 up but Douglas had strayed offside and Burnley breathed again.

The Clarets drew level midway through the second half when the ball dropped loose to McILROY who hit it first time through a thickly populated goalmouth and past the unsighted Leyland. As Burnley pressed forward, Matt Woods nearly sliced the ball into his own net. Dobing should have scored for Rovers and Connelly nearly did so for Burnley. There were just two minutes left when ROBSON overcame the Rovers defence to head home the winning goal from Connelly's corner kick.

Then Robson was through again – he dummied the goalkeeper and shot into the net – but the whistle had gone for offside. However, he had put the Clarets into the next round and at the final whistle, he was engulfed in a wave of claret and blue.

Blackburn Rovers
H. Leyland; K. Taylor; W. Eckersley; R. Clayton; M. Woods; M. McGrath; B. Douglas; P. Dobing; T. Johnson; R. Vernon; A. MacLeod

Burnley
C. McDonald; T. Cummings; D. Smith; R. Seith; B. Miller; J. Adamson; J. Connelly; J. McIlroy; R. Pointer; J. Robson; B. Pilkington

Attendance: 43,752

Match 100
7 March 1959
Blackburn Rovers 4 Burnley 1

The Ewood Park game was not a classic – 'Derby' matches seldom reach such heights – but Rovers went about their job in a more convincing manner, demonstrating the values of being able to shoot from any angle and any reasonable distance.

Yet it was Burnley who took the lead after 20 minutes when a Robson-Seith-Connelly move saw Leyland push out a long in-swinging centre to POINTER who promptly smashed it back past the Rovers 'keeper for the game's opening goal.

The home side almost equalised a minute later when a Bryan Douglas cross shot beat Blacklaw's dive, cracked the far post and rebounded into play. Rovers equalised in the 33rd minute when DOBING shot through a crowd of players past the Clarets unsighted 'keeper. STEPHENSON put Rovers 2-1 up just before half-time when he accepted a sharp pass from Dobing before smacking the ball into the roof of the net past a surprised Blacklaw.

Burnley did better after the interval but despite the pressure, they had nothing to show for it and the goal came at the other end instead. Clayton and Douglas worked the ball into the area where AIREY had the simple task of side-Footing the ball past Blacklaw.

VERNON got Rovers' fourth goal from a Stephenson pass and could have added a fifth if he had not shot over when put through by Clayton.

Blackburn Rovers
H. Leyland; K. Taylor; D. Whelan; R. Clayton; M. Woods; M. McGrath;
B. Douglas; R. Stephenson; P. Dobing; R. Vernon; J. Airey

Burnley
A. Blacklaw; T. Cummings; D. Smith; R. Seith; B. Miller; J. Adamson;
J. Connelly; J. McIlroy; R. Pointer; J. Robson; B. Pilkington

Attendance: 27,071

Match 101
17 October 1959
Blackburn Rovers 3 Burnley 2

Though the match could not be described as a memorable 'Derby' it certainly had incident with both sides enjoying periods of ascendancy.

It was a sudden beating of three men and a short forward pass which led to Rovers taking the lead – a beautiful shot taken in his stride by Northern Ireland international centre-forward, Derek DOUGAN. Play was fast without being particularly exciting and the participants mixed it with some tough tackling.

Burnley's period of ascendancy was emphasised by a deserved equaliser. A Seith-McIlroy free-kick act resulted in PILKINGTON shooting in at the back post. However, Rovers won back the initiative largely through Dobing's speedy penetrations and they regained the lead. With everyone expecting him to pass, DOBING fired in a hard, angled shot which curled over the outstretched arms of Adam Blacklaw and under the bar.

Shortly after half-time, Pointer almost equalised with an overhead kick and then White shot straight at Harry Leyland.

Burnley's second goal also came from a free-kick. This time, Miller added variety by turning it square to Seith whose shot rebounded to DOUGLAS. In an inglorious attempt at a back pass, the England winger curled the ball over Leyland under the bar and into his own net!

Now on level terms, Burnley looked as if they would snatch the winner. However, it was Rovers' Roy VERNON who came up trumps. He lobbed a free-kick over the defensive wall and as Dougan moved to meet the ball with his leg raised, Blacklaw seemed to lose the line of flight completely and the ball ended up in the net.

Still the Clarets could have equalised but Harry Leyland saved his side with two split-second diversions late in the game.

Blackburn Rovers
H. Leyland; J. Bray; F. Pickering; W. Smith; M. Woods; M. McGrath;
B. Douglas; P. Dobing; D. Dougan; R. Vernon; A. MacLeod

Burnley
A. Blacklaw; J. Angus; A. Elder; R. Seith; J. Adamson; B. Miller;
B. Pilkington; J. McIlroy; R. Pointer; W. White; G. Harris

Attendance: 33,316

Match 102
5 March 1960
Burnley 1 Blackburn Rovers 0

Both sides played with an excessive amount of caution, so much so that the spectators could be excused for thinking that they were saving the 'fireworks' for the coming Saturday's FA Cup tie.

It was a disappointing 'Derby' to say the least with both sides wanting to give little away! The highlight of the opening exchanges saw Ronnie Clayton send a shot crashing against the foot of Blacklaw's right-hand post before being scrambled to safety by Angus and Dougan loop a header onto the roof of the Burnley 'keeper's net.

ROBSON scored for Burnley midway through the first half after good work on the right by John Connelly. The Burnley winger almost extended his side's lead early in the second half from a corner given away by Whelan when he dropped a shot on top of the crossbar.

Blacklaw had more to do in the final ten minutes than he had in the previous eighty, as Rovers went in search of an equaliser. Ally MacLeod sent in a powerful drive that the Burnley 'keeper kicked out on the volley, thus giving the crowd one of the few laughs on a grim afternoon.

Burnley
A. Blacklaw; J. Angus; A. Elder; R. Seith; B. Miller; J. Adamson;
J. Connelly; J. McIlroy; R. Pointer; J. Robson; B. Pilkington

Blackburn Rovers
H. Leyland; J. Bray; D. Whelan; R. Clayton; M. Woods; M. McGrath;
B. Douglas; P. Dobing; D. Dougan; E. Thomas; A. MacLeod

Attendance: 32,331

Match 103
12 March 1960
Burnley 3 Blackburn Rovers 3

This sixth round FA Cup tie had everything – tremendous excitement, fluctuating fortune and spectacular goals, all watched by a crowd of 51,501.

Although the first half was goalless, the visitors had had enough of the play to suggest that it would only be a matter of time before they took the lead. In fact, if Scottish international goalkeeper Adam Blacklaw hadn't been at his best, Rovers would have finished the first half at least two goals to the good.

However, the opening stages of the second half were a completely different story. Led by Jimmy McIlroy, the Clarets seized the initiative and took the lead when the Irishman's crossfield pass found Brian PILKINGTON and his right-foot shot flew wide of Harry Leyland's despairing dive, entering the net at the angle of crossbar and post. Encouraged by this success, the Clarets began to get on top and extended their lead when POINTER was left with a simple tap-in following good work along the by-line by McIlroy. In an unbelievable turn around, John CONNELLY made it 3-0 for Burnley when his speed took him past two Rovers defenders before slipping the ball past the advancing Leyland.

There were just fifteen minutes left when a harmless shot by Peter Dobing that appeared to be going well wide, flew up and struck Alex Elder's hand. Though it looked completely unintentional, the referee awarded a penalty, from which Bryan DOUGLAS made no mistake.

Three minutes later, Rovers reduced the arrears again when DOBING from fully 25 yards out, beat Blacklaw with a powerfully hit shot.

In the remaining minutes, the Burnley defence came under an awful amount of pressure and with just four minutes remaining, Clayton's long hopeful punt upfield found the unmarked Mick McGRATH. Though he sliced his shot, it beat Blacklaw, hit the inside of the post and rolled into the net!

Burnley
A. Blacklaw; J. Angus; A. Elder; R. Seith; B. Miller; J. Adamson; J. Connelly; J. McIlroy; R. Pointer; J. Robson; B. Pilkington

Blackburn Rovers
H. Leyland; J. Bray; D. Whelan; R. Clayton; M. Woods; M. McGrath; L. Bimpson; P. Dobing; D. Dougan; B. Douglas; A. MacLeod

Attendance: 51,501

Match 104
16 March 1960
Blackburn Rovers 2 Burnley 0

Nerves played an early part in this FA Cup replay with bad passes, mistimed tackles, body checks and even the good old-fashioned rugby 'hand-off' as the teams tried to settle down.

When Northern Ireland international colleagues, Dougan and McIlroy went for a 50-50 ball, the big Rovers centre-forward was carried off. Word reached the Press Box that he would be resuming after the interval but he delayed his return until the teams were out. His fine sense of the dramatic was rewarded with a mighty cheer from the home supporters, whilst McIlroy, who had received a lecture for his part in the incident, was booed until it was all forgotten!

The second half deteriorated into a scrappy affair and with both sides unable to produce a goal, the game went into extra-time. Dougan shot through a crowded penalty area from a Douglas squared free-kick to which DOBING got his head. This goal brought on hordes of whooping Rovers fans to engulf the Burnley goal, with the result that the ball was temporarily 'lost' before order was restored.

Burnley desperately tried to force an equaliser, pushing Miller up into attack but this brought with it the danger of breakaway raids. Rovers emphasised their superiority with a second goal. A long throw-in from Clayton was met by the head of MacLEOD who looped the ball over the outstretched arms of Adam Blacklaw.

A minute from time, the referee blew for an infringement and this brought a wholesale invasion of the pitch from the crowded Darwen End, but it only served to prolong the proceedings for a few extra minutes as Rovers won through to the semi-final.

Blackburn Rovers
H. Leyland; J. Bray; D. Whelan; R. Clayton; M. Woods; M. McGrath; L. Bimpson; P. Dobing; D. Dougan; B. Douglas; A. MacLeod

Burnley
A. Blacklaw; J. Angus; A. Elder; R. Seith; B. Miller; J. Adamson; J. Connelly; J. McIlroy; R. Pointer; J. Robson; B. Pilkington

Attendance: 53,839

Match 105
8 October 1960
Blackburn Rovers 1 Burnley 4

The Northern Ireland v England international in Belfast robbed both sides of their star players. Rovers were without Douglas and Dougan whilst the Clarets were missing the talents of McIlroy, Elder and Miller.

Burnley had the better of the early exchanges with Ray Pointer dangerous every time he moved out to the wing and the first goal came from one of his centres after Robson and Angus had prompted the move. CONNELLY nipped in to finish it in the 19th minute but four minutes later, Rovers were level when EDDIE THOMAS completed a similar move with Crowe supplying the centre from the right-wing.

In the vital minutes before the interval, CONNELLY restored the Clarets' lead before McGrath smashed a shot against Blacklaw's crossbar with the Aberdeen-born 'keeper well beaten. Isherwood did likewise in the first minute of the second half and Rovers supporters must have been convinced it was not their day when Dobing tried a snap-shot and nearly hit the corner flag!

Burnley extended their lead when Woods failed to resist the temptation to use his hand to stop a near-post shot from Connelly, which looked as if it was going wide. ADAMSON made no mistake from the spot, sending Jones the wrong way.

Four minutes from time, ROBSON added his name to the scoresheet with a great low shot from Pilkington's pin-point cross.

Blackburn Rovers
R. Jones; M. England; F. Pickering; R. Clayton; M. Woods; M. McGrath; R. Isherwood; E. Thomas; P. Dobing; C. Crowe; A. MacLeod

Burnley
A. Blacklaw; J. Angus; W. Marshall; W. Joyce; T. Cummings; J. Adamson; J. Connelly; J. Robson; R. Pointer; G. Harris; B. Pilkington

Attendance: 26,223

Match 106
25 February 1961
Burnley 1 Blackburn Rovers 1

Though both sets of players deserved praise for their attempts to provide football entertainment for their respective supporters who had braved the damp and drizzle, the only incident of note in a goalless first half was provided by a dog. It decided to investigate the antics of these strangely clad humans, obviously feeling it could do better with its four feet than what the players were trying to do with two! As play stopped, the animal allowed itself to be soothed by the Ulster blarney of Alex Elder after referee Arthur Ellis had attempted to tackle it from behind! It must have thought that it was about to have its name taken and promptly nipped the official before being placed under arrest!

More heavy rain made the ball even more difficult to move – Dobing and Harris did it at speed with fast dribbles whilst Matt Woods thumped it out of the middle morass whenever it came his way. Both McIlroy and Pointer tasted mud after attempts to carry attacks down the centre and the Northern Ireland international missed a chance from the latter's cross.

However, the Clarets took the lead in the 61st minute with Joyce, Elder, Harris and Robson making the running and MILLER confounding the Rovers defence by racing through to head the ball wide of Leyland. From the kick-off, Rovers made progress down the left where they were awarded a free-kick. Ally MacLEOD levelled the scores, turning home Clayton's kick. The Rovers skipper then hit the outside of Blacklaw's left-hand post before Thomas completely missed his kick with just the Burnley 'keeper to beat. Both sides pressed hard for the winner but in the end the only winner were the conditions.

Burnley
A. Blacklaw; J. Angus; A. Elder; W. Joyce; J. Adamson; B. Miller; J. Connelly; J. McIlroy; R. Pointer; J. Robson; G. Harris

Blackburn Rovers
H. Leyland; K. Taylor; J. Bray; A. McEvoy; M. Woods; R. Clayton; B. Douglas; P. Dobing; D. Dougan; E. Thomas; A. MacLeod

Attendance: 26,492

Match 107
24 February 1962
Blackburn Rovers 2 Burnley 1

There were only three things worthy of note in the first 45 minutes. The first was Burnley's goal scored after 27 minutes when Connelly's accurate right-wing corner was headed back across the face of Blackburn's goal by Towers for POINTER to head wide of Else's right-hand into the corner of the net. There was an isolated piece of juggling by Jimmy McIlroy which bordered on football genius and the keenness, determination and will-to-succeed of 19-year-old Ian Towers who had come in as a last-minute deputy for the injured Gordon Harris. Though Burnley were the better of two very disappointing sides in the first half, it was a different story after the interval.

Within 75 seconds of the restart, LAWTHER had levelled the scores. Douglas' square pass was pushed on by Pickering to Lawther who gave Blacklaw no chance with a low, hard-hit 18-yard drive.

Perhaps the biggest miss of the afternoon came on the hour mark when Eddie Thomas, who was deputising for John Byrom, found himself clean through after a superb piece of work by Douglas. Thomas however, wasted a gilt-edged opportunity by shooting straight at Blacklaw. Rovers 'keeper Fred Else made one excellent save from Robson and then the lanky inside-left shot wide after good work by McIlroy. Later Else made a good save from Ray Pointer's 25-yard drive. Rovers took the lead when an immaculate pass by Clayton found Lawther in space and his cross was headed in off a post by Fred PICKERING.

The Clarets almost snatched a late equaliser when Towers intercepted a back-pass by Newton. He squared the ball across Rovers' unguarded goal but with Pointer limping, there wasn't a forward quick enough to be on the spot to turn a glorious chance into what would have been a certain goal!

Blackburn Rovers
F. Else; K. Taylor; K. Newton; R. Clayton; M. Woods; M. McGrath; B. Douglas; I. Lawther; F. Pickering; E. Thomas; B. Ratcliffe

Burnley
A. Blacklaw; J. Angus; A. Elder; J. Adamson; T. Cummings; B. Miller; J. Connelly; J. McIlroy; R. Pointer; J. Robson; I. Towers

Attendance: 33,914

Match 108
17 April 1962
Burnley 0 Blackburn Rovers 1

A solitary goal by Rovers outside-right Barrie Ratcliffe gave the visitors a 1-0 win and took away two more valuable points from the Clarets who were bidding to win their third Football League Championship.

Burnley had only themselves to blame for letting Rovers become the only team to complete the 'double' over them that season. The Clarets threw away chance after chance as the Rovers goal led a charmed life.

However, Blackburn could have taken the lead as early as the fifth minute as Talbut slipped and Fred Pickering raced clear only to shoot into the side-netting. The Burnley centre-half soon made amends with a pin-point cross to Ray Pointer who tested Bob Jones with a stinging shot from fully 40-yards. John Connelly hit the post with a pile-drive but after 31 minutes, Rovers stunned the home crowd when RATCLIFFE scored from a pass by Lawther.

In the second half, it was all one-way traffic as Burnley pressed forward in search of an equaliser. Jones scrambled McIlroy's shot to safety and then saved magnificently from Connelly.

An equalising goal seemed on the cards but Rovers hung on to claim a famous victory.

Burnley
A. Blacklaw; J. Angus; A. Elder; J. Adamson; T. Cummings; W. Joyce; J. Connelly; J. McIlroy; R. Pointer; J. Robson; I. Towers

Blackburn Rovers
R. Jones; K. Taylor; K. Newton; R. Clayton; M. England; M. McGrath; B. Ratcliffe; I. Lawther; F. Pickering; B. Douglas; J. Haverty

Attendance: 29,997

Match 109
6 October 1962
Blackburn Rovers 2 Burnley 3

Several times in the first half-hour of this East Lancashire Derby, Rovers centre-forward Fred Pickering was given time and room to collect the ball and get into his stride before any kind of challenge was made. So therefore it was not altogether surprising when after neat work by Clayton, Pickering slipped speedily through the Burnley defence to lay on the first goal in the 22nd minute. Pulling the ball back from the by-line, Pickering found LAWTHER who stabbed the ball home from five yards.

After a number of short corners, Connelly decided to centre directly and Else, with plenty of time at his disposal, carelessly fisted the ball away but only to HARRIS who scored with a good left-foot drive. Within two minutes, LOCHHEAD had given Burnley the lead after a move involving Angus, Pointer and McIlroy. The Clarets were in command as the first half drew to a close, a measure of their superiority being the seven corners they won while conceding none. Yet, within four minutes of the restart, Rovers were level when Talbut was adjudged to have handled Lawther's cross and DOUGLAS scored from the spot.

Again it didn't take Burnley long to regain the lead, for in the 52nd minute, LOCHHEAD played a neat one-two with Harris before firing past Else in the Blackburn goal. That was the end of the scoring but not of the incident as Rovers' Bryan Douglas and Burnley's Andy Lochhead came in for a lot of rough treatment, resulting in a number of players from both sides having their names taken.

Blackburn Rovers
F. Else; J. Bray; K. Newton; R. Clayton; M. Woods; M. McGrath; B. Douglas; I. Lawther; F. Pickering; R. Craig; M. Harrison

Burnley
A. Blacklaw; J. Angus; A. Elder; J. Adamson; J. Talbut; B. Miller; J. Connelly; R. Pointer; A. Lochhead; J. McIlroy; G. Harris

Attendance: 26,626

Match 110
2 April 1963
Burnley 1 Blackburn Rovers 0

Burnley recorded their first League 'double' of the season when they beat Blackburn Rovers 1-0 through a 37th-minute penalty by Gordon Harris.

The only disappointment, which anyone could derive from this 'Derby', was that in a match of so much determination by both sides to get goals, the result should be decided by a penalty. So many chances and goalworthy attempts were made that goalkeepers Blacklaw and Else were kept busy throughout the game.

In three ferocious minutes between the 19th and 21st, Else made brilliant saves from Miller and Harris. Blacklaw picked another potential winner from Pickering out of the bottom corner and then took a swerving drive from Byrom in the style, which was to continue the pattern of goalkeeping throughout the ninety minutes. Counting the woodwork and the chances Burnley missed, there wasn't a forward without some guilt and even allowing for Mike England's header which grazed the bar late on, Burnley had the edge on things that might have been.

Goalkeeping performances apart, the highlight of the match was the outstanding wing-play of Gordon Harris. He linked up splendidly with Bellamy whilst for Rovers, centre-half Matt Woods was a tower of strength. He refused to be drawn out of position despite the efforts that Andy Lochhead made to entice him.

The goal came about after HARRIS' thunderbolt had come back off the bar and struck Keith Newton on the hand – an unfortunate but nevertheless guilty offence!

It was a good game, one of the few 'Derby' games that has been full of excitement for fans, whilst another feature was that neither trainer had to be called on at any part of the game.

Burnley
A. Blacklaw; J. Angus; M. Buxton; D. Walker; J. Talbut; B. Miller; J. Connelly; R. Pointer; A. Lochhead; A. Bellamy; G. Harris

Blackburn Rovers
F. Else; J. Bray; K. Newton; R. Clayton; M. Woods; M. England; B. Douglas; A. McEvoy; F. Pickering; J. Byrom; M. Harrison

Attendance: 25,746

Match 111
1 October 1963
Burnley 3 Blackburn Rovers 0

The 'Derby' match which flared into a rough house ended with the Clarets beating Rovers 3-0 and it was sixty seconds of drama which wrecked the Ewood Park club. Fighting hard to pull back a one goal deficit, Rovers were stunned when centre-half Mike England was sent off and shattered the moment play restarted when Burnley grabbed a second goal.

It was the Clarets who played with a real urgency and a will to win and it was no surprise when they took the lead. Lochhead flicked on a Blacklaw clearance and BELLAMY left Else helpless with a left-foot volley. The ill-feeling crept in during the 17th minute when John Talbut and Fred Pickering were both spoken to by the referee. Then in a further flash of petulance after 28 minutes, Brian O'Neill fouled Bryan Douglas and almost immediately the England winger returned the compliment!

The referee had his work cut out as in a ten-minute spell early in the second half, Talbut and Pickering had their names taken following a clash and England was booked for another foul on Lochhead. Then three minutes later, England again brought down Lochhead after the Burnley man had beaten him and it was no less than the referee could do but to send the Welsh international off. The marching orders for England sparked off sixty seconds which shattered the Rovers, for from the resulting free-kick, BELLAMY scored his and Burnley's second goal with a free header.

Burnley now dictated the game against a Rovers side which relied mainly on Douglas. The Clarets extended their lead in the 78th minute when Bellamy's centre was met by JOYCE who beat Else's desperate dive to find the corner of the net. The difference between the sides was the advantage Burnley held at half-back with Brian Miller outstanding both as captain and player.

Burnley
A. Blacklaw; J. Angus; W. Joyce; B. O'Neill; J. Talbut; B. Miller; T. Meredith; A. Bellamy; A. Lochhead; J. Robson; J. Connelly

Blackburn Rovers
F. Else; J. Bray; K. Newton; R. Clayton; M. England; A. McEvoy; B. Ratcliffe; J. Byrom; F. Pickering; B. Douglas; M. Harrison

Attendance: 24,345

Match 112
19 October 1963
Blackburn Rovers 1 Burnley 2

Burnley were well on top at the start and went very close to scoring when Lochhead's cross was headed over his own bar by Andy McEvoy. From the resulting corner, Miller headed narrowly wide. Burnley continued to press and when Angus beat Douglas in a race for the ball, his cross was met by Bellamy, his shot hitting the underside of the bar with Else well beaten.

Rovers eventually got their game together and when Angus slipped, Harrison's deep cross was taken off Byrom's toes as the youngster seemed certain to score. Burnley came back again – they had been the more dangerous by far, moving the ball quickly and imaginatively. However, it was Rovers who took the lead after 19 minutes after Lochhead had given away a free-kick just inside the Burnley half. England lobbed a long kick forward and PICKERING outjumped Talbut to head the ball out of Blacklaw's reach.

It was all Rovers now, Pickering beat Talbut on the ground but instead of closing in for a shot, he came back with the ball to try and beat Talbut again and was robbed. From Clayton's beautifully weighted pass, Ferguson hit a scorching drive which Blacklaw did well to turn round the post.

The Scottish international 'keeper was in action again soon after, turning over a 30-yard drive from Harrison. A smart interception by Miller prevented Byrom from adding to Rovers' lead. Though the Burnley defence was under a great deal of pressure, they managed to hold out until half-time.

Byrom almost scored in the opening minutes of the second half but his angled drive scraped the outside of Blacklaw's right-hand post. Burnley equalised against the run of play in the 58th minute when Bellamy pulled the ball back for CONNELLY to beat Else from close in. Burnley escaped dramatically when Douglas had a shot charged down by Talbut in a frantic goalmouth scramble and then Pickering following up, shot straight at Blacklaw. The Clarets forced two quick corners and from the second, Bray blocked the ball on the line. Harris twice went close with long-range shots before at the other end, Clayton brought a magnificent save out of Blacklaw, the Burnley 'keeper tipping the ball over the bar at the last minute. After 83 minutes, Burnley moved into the lead when Meredith's cross was met by CONNELLY and from an acute angle, the winger beat Else's despairing dive.

In the dying minutes, Clayton headed over from Douglas' cross and with time running out, Rovers claimed for a penalty for handball against Buxton but the referee would have nothing of it.

Blackburn Rovers
F. Else; J. Bray; K. Newton; R. Clayton; M. England; M. McGrath; M. Ferguson; A. McEvoy; F. Pickering; B. Douglas; M. Harrison

Burnley
A. Blacklaw; J. Angus; M. Buxton; B. O'Neill; J. Talbut; B. Miller; T. Meredith; A. Bellamy; A. Lochhead; G. Harris; J. Connelly

Attendance: 26,740

Match 113
10 October 1964
Burnley 1 Blackburn Rovers 1

After a first half in which the defences dominated, the game flared into action but there were still more flashes of temper and lectures by the referee to players of both sides than real thrills.

Burnley's Willie Morgan had the game's first chance but after rounding Jones, he put the ball into the crowd! Price almost opened the scoring but his shot having beaten Else, went just outside the post. Todd twice won applause for the way he policed Douglas and it was the Northern Ireland international who fed Irvine, forcing Else to dive at his feet and knock the ball for a corner. After 19 minutes there was a scare for the Rovers as Joyce mis-hit a back-pass straight to Irvine who was brought down unceremoniously. Burnley players appealed for a penalty but the referee gave a free-kick on the edge of the penalty area. Following this, the ball went to Todd who shot inches wide from 30 yards out. Rovers' best chance of the first half fell to Andy McEvoy whose shot on the turn beat Blacklaw but was deflected for a corner by Alex Elder.

The second half opened with both defences having no trouble in coping with the respective attacks. Then all of a sudden, Clayton, Ferguson and Douglas contrived to make a chance for Bradshaw but he was thwarted by Blacklaw who dived bravely at his feet to claim the ball. Angus pushed the ball through to Towers and when he centred, Clayton appeared to handle but again the referee ignored the Clarets' claims. Irvine then hit the side-netting from a pass by Price and Towers shot over the bar with Else prostate on the ground.

In a game littered with fouls, two penalties were awarded in the final few minutes, one for each side. Angus was pulled up for handling as DOUGLAS flicked the ball through and it was the Rovers winger who scored from the spot. There were just two minutes left to play when Morgan was brought down by Joyce and though Else got his finger tips to LOCHHEAD's penalty, he couldn't prevent it from entering the net.

Burnley
A. Blacklaw; J. Angus; A. Elder; S. Todd; J. Talbut; B. Miller; W. Morgan; W. Irvine; A. Lochhead; I. Towers; J. Price

Blackburn Rovers
F. Else; K. Newton; W. Joyce; R. Clayton; M. England; M. McGrath; M. Ferguson; A. McEvoy; J. Byrom; B. Douglas; A. Bradshaw

Attendance: 21,199

Match 114
24 February 1965
Blackburn Rovers 1 Burnley 4

Burnley dominated the game throughout and even before Rovers full-back Billy Wilson left the field with a leg injury in the 34th minute, Blackburn looked on the way to yet another home defeat.

Up to this point, Blacklaw had far his quietest game of the season and the only home forward to have a shot at goal was John Byrom. His best effort – a shot on the run – was well saved by Blacklaw and in another rare Rovers attack, Angus cleared a Byrom header off the line.

Burnley took the lead after 40 minutes when Elder put a crossfield pass to Towers and his centre was fired into the roof of the net by IRVINE. A minute before half-time, ELDER tried another pass from the edge of the penalty area and when the ball bounced back to him off England, the left-back drove it past Fred Else.

Burnley spent most of the second half camped in the Rovers half of the pitch. Bellamy was in tremendous form and was the driving force behind the Clarets' non-stop pressure. Else in the home goal made half-a-dozen top-class saves, the best from Andy Lochhead.

With ten minutes remaining, England brought down Towers and from the resultant free-kick, O'NEILL scored with a fierce shot. Five minutes later, Rovers pulled a goal back when Douglas, who had switched to the left-wing, crossed for McGRATH to score with a first-time shot.

In the 89th minute, a terrific right-wing run and cross by Bellamy gave IRVINE the simple task of side-footing home Burnley's fourth goal.

Blackburn Rovers
F. Else; W. Wilson; W. Joyce; R. Clayton; M. England; M. McGrath; M. Ferguson; A. McEvoy; J. Byrom; B. Douglas; M. Harrison

Burnley
A. Blacklaw; J. Angus; A. Elder; B. O'Neill; J. Talbut; B. Miller; I. Towers; W. Irvine; A. Lochhead; A. Bellamy; L. Latcham

Attendance: 15,340

Match 115
9 October 1965
Burnley 1 Blackburn Rovers 4

Burnley started the game among the League leaders and were unbeaten at home whilst Rovers were the First Division's bottom club, without an away win! The visitors took the lead after 16 minutes when stand-in centre-forward MIKE ENGLAND beat John Talbut to the ball to shoot past Thomson. After this goal, the Clarets defence became more and more jittery and more and more disorganised. A minute later, Rovers went 2-0 up when a bad pass by Bellamy allowed Douglas to make progress down the right-wing before crossing for HARRISON to head home.

Burnley looked very lethargic and though Andy LOCHHEAD made it 2-1, it was no surprise when McEVOY got a third for Rovers on the half-hour mark, the ball going into the net via the post. Blackburn could have had a bigger interval lead, Miller clearing off the line from Harrison and Elder repeating the rescue act when Douglas followed up with another shot on target.

For a time in the second half, Burnley laid siege to the Rovers goal and Fred Else made a couple of breathtaking saves from O'Neill and Harris. Irvine missed the best chance when put clean through, then Rovers got into their stride again. O'Neill conceded a free-kick, Joyce crossed, England headed on and as Thomson made an effort to grab the ball, DOUGLAS swept it over the line.

In the first half, the Burnley 'keeper was under fire from both directions. He faced the Blackburn goal barrage and stood with his back to the bombardment from the terraces from where fireworks, bottles and two large steel bolts were thrown!

Burnley
H. Thomson; J. Angus; A. Elder; B. O'Neill; J. Talbut; B. Miller; W. Morgan; A. Lochhead; W. Irvine; G. Harris; A. Bellamy

Blackburn Rovers
F. Else; W. Wilson; W. Joyce; R. Clayton; R. Mulvaney; G. Sharples; M. Ferguson; A. McEvoy; M. England; B. Douglas; M. Harrison

Attendance: 23,198

Match 116
1 January 1966
Blackburn Rovers 0 Burnley 2

In a hard-fought 'Derby' vital for both sides but for different reasons, Burnley took the points. The Clarets made the first real threat when Irvine headed the ball back into the path of Harris, whose shot went inches wide of Else's right-hand upright. Clayton then stopped Coates in his tracks before Darling's misplaced pass set up Brian O'Neill, his shot bringing a fine save out of Else. At the other end, Ferguson was fouled and took the free-kick, sending a quick pass to Jones, who was well tackled by Todd as he was about to get in a shot. Irvine then shot straight at Else and Mike England's header brought a fine save out of Blacklaw. The miss of the match came in the 16th minute when Jones cleverly took the ball round Blacklaw, then shot wide of an empty goal from five yards out.

Burnley took the lead when O'Neill turned his free-kick sideways and Elder hit a cracking drive, which Else turned against the post. The ball then bounced across the face of the goal and IRVINE was the first to react, turning the ball over the line before Else could recover. Rovers hit back strongly with both Darling and England going close, the latter's header grazing the bar with Blacklaw beaten. In the dying moments of the first half, England headed the ball to Jones whose glancing header lacked power and Blacklaw saved comfortably.

Early in the second half, Harrison cut inside Angus but sliced his shot from a narrow angle that was well wide. Clayton twice broke up promising Burnley attacks before Morgan flashed across the face of the Rovers goal where Irvine was only inches short of connecting and sliding the ball past Else. Burnley went further ahead in the 68th minute when Coates turned the ball back to HARRIS whose drive from 25 yards skidded, gathered pace and beat Else. Eight minutes from the end, the game erupted when Morgan was sent off for a foul on England. A minute later, a spectator dashed from behind the Rovers goal after Blacklaw had been involved in an incident with England and began grappling with the Burnley 'keeper. Two policeman separated them before removing the youth. It was a stormy and sensational end to a game which had never threatened ill-feeling until the dying moments.

Blackburn Rovers
F. Else; K. Newton; W. Wilson; R. Clayton; R. Mulvaney; G. Sharples; M. Darling; G. Jones; M. England; M. Ferguson; M. Harrison

Burnley
A. Blacklaw; J. Angus; A. Elder; B. O'Neill; B. Miller; S. Todd; W. Morgan; A. Bellamy; W. Irvine; G. Harris; R. Coates

Attendance: 28,013

Match 117
7 August 1976
Blackburn Rovers 1 Burnley 1

Blackburn had the best of the early play in this Anglo-Scottish Cup tie and Fazackerley forced a good save out of Peyton as early as the third minute. The Rovers defender also came close with a powerful header which went inches wide with the Burnley 'keeper beaten. Burnley replied with three good attempts on goal. Noble headed over from six yards after good work by Newton, then the same player had another header saved by Bradshaw before Hankin, too, saw his header taken by the Rovers 'keeper.

Stuart Metcalfe produced one of the best shots of the game with a powerful 20-yard drive in the 35th minute, which Peyton saved well. The Clarets took the lead two minutes before the interval when FLYNN sprinted onto a return pass from Hankin before looping the ball over Paul Bradshaw.

The visitors had strong claims for a penalty early in the second half when Fazackerley appeared to bring down Flynn and then Bradshaw had to race out of his goal to block a shot by Noble. Hankin then sent in a 30-yard effort, which whistled past Bradshaw's left-hand upright. However, as the game entered the last quarter-of-an-hour, Blackburn came strongly into the picture and Peyton was forced into making good saves from Metcalfe and Parkes before the equaliser came in the 84th minute. WAGSTAFFE cut in diagonally from the wing past Scott and exchanged passes with Bobby Svarc before shooting past Peyton.

Billy Ingham had a last-minute chance to give victory to Burnley but he shot past the post after Hankin had knocked down substitute Loggie's pin-point cross.

Blackburn Rovers
P. Bradshaw; J. Waddington; J. Bailey; S. Metcalfe; D. Fazackerley; G. Hawkins; G. Taylor; K. Hird; A. Needham; T. Parkes; D. Wagstaffe

Burnley
G. Peyton; D. Scott; K. Newton; P. Noble; J. Thomson; B. Rodaway; C. Morris; R. Hankin; W. Ingham; B. Flynn (D. Loggie); M. Summerbee

Attendance: 11,012

Match 118
27 December 1976
Blackburn Rovers 2 Burnley 2

Though this was the first draw in a total of ten 'Derby' clashes at Ewood Park since the war, even the most ardent Clarets fans would concede that they were lucky to grab a point from a one-sided game.

Bobby Svarc nearly opened the scoring when he threw himself acrobatically to Tony Parkes' cross and missed connecting with the ball by a whisker. Byrom then shot into the side-netting as Rovers mounted attack after attack. Stuart Metcalfe forced Alan Stevenson into making a number of fine saves, the best a 25-yard free-kick that forced the Clarets 'keeper to tip over the bar. A clever chip by Byrom was held by Stevenson above his head whilst Metcalfe was just off target with a shot from the edge of the area. Stevenson was a very busy man and he saved involuntary from Parkes to concede a corner. From the flag kick, Byrom hit a post. It had been all Rovers but Burnley nearly took the lead when Bradshaw was left stranded by a back pass from Alcock.

After a goalless first half, Rovers took the lead in the 52nd minute when John BYROM turned in Wagstaffe's corner at the near post. The home side's second goal came ten minutes later when Wagstaffe's drive came back to him off a defensive wall and this time he threaded the ball through for BYROM to score his and Rovers' second goal. Byrom took both these chances with a minimum of effort but the maximum of efficiency.

The turning point in the game came when Rovers lost Gordon Taylor with a badly bruised shin – the home side was thrown into a state of inbalance and Burnley took the opportunity to move forward. They pulled one back in the 80th minute when, following Keith Newton's shot hitting a post, NOBLE followed up to score off the underside of the bar. The equaliser came with just two minutes left as the referee ignored the linesman's flag and allowed Brian Flynn to cross for Ian BRENNAN to hammer the ball into the net through a crowd of defenders.

Blackburn Rovers
P. Bradshaw; K. Hird; J. Bailey; S. Metcalfe; J. Waddington; T. Alcock; G. Taylor (N. Wilkinson); R. Svarc; J. Byrom; T. Parkes; D. Wagstaffe

Burnley
A. Stevenson; K. Newton; I. Brennan; P. Noble; J. Thomson; B. Rodaway; T. Cochrane; M. Smith; P. Fletcher (T. Morley); B. Flynn; W. Ingham

Attendance: 22,189

Match 119
8 April 1977
Burnley 3 Blackburn Rovers 1

With Rovers looking decidedly lethargic, the Clarets appeared to be on their way to a comfortable victory when Malcolm SMITH gave them the lead in the sixth minute. The five-man build-up to the goal was finished off neatly when Smith turned on Brian Flynn's pass to hammer a 12-yard shot wide of Bradshaw.

Robinson, Fletcher and Morley all went close as the Clarets penned the visitors back and could have put the outcome beyond doubt. But as the half wore on, Rovers came back into the game and equalised a minute before the interval. The goal was set up by Wagstaffe, whose pin-point centre was headed into the goalmouth by Parkes and from the resulting melee, SVARC forced the ball home.

Midway through the second half, a defensive lapse by Waddington, who carelessly headed Fletcher's deep cross across the penalty area, the ball falling at the feet of Peter NOBLE who drove his shot beyond Bradshaw.

Burnley netted a third goal six minutes from time when from a well-worked corner-kick move, Noble flicked on Morley's flag-kick for 19-year-old centre-half Peter ROBINSON to curl a header over the stranded Bradshaw. Three players were booked in a flurry of activity during an eight-minute spell in the second half but, if anything, the tackling was quite tame by Derby-match standards!

Burnley
A. Stevenson; K. Newton; I. Brennan; P. Noble; P. Robinson; B. Rodaway; T. Cochrane; M. Smith; P. Fletcher; B. Flynn; T. Morley

Blackburn Rovers
P. Bradshaw; K. Hird; J. Bailey; G. Keeley; J. Waddington; G. Hawkins; S. Metcalfe; G. Taylor; R. Svarc (M. Wood); T. Parkes; D. Wagstaffe

Attendance: 17, 372

Match 120
2 August 1977
Burnley 2 Blackburn Rovers 1

The Clarets dominated the first half of this Anglo-Scottish Cup match and it would have been no injustice if they had turned round two or three goals ahead at the interval. Instead they had to content themselves with a 1-0 lead thanks to Malcolm SMITH's cheeky seventh-minute chip which deceived Rovers 'keeper Paul Bradshaw and found the net via the far post.

Fletcher missed a great chance to increase the home side's lead when he mistimed a header in front of goal. Bradshaw produced a fine full-length save from Smith's 25-yard drive as Burnley kept up the pressure.

The second half was an entirely different story even though Burnley went further ahead after 59 minutes when Cochrane and Flynn split the right side of the Rovers defence for the Welsh international's low cross to be forced home by INGHAM. Blackburn came close to reducing the deficit in the 67th minute when Newton cleared Metcalfe's 18-yard drive off the line and then Stevenson brilliantly turned aside a shot from Tony Parkes. Rovers pulled a goal back in the 75th minute when Brotherston turned the ball across goal for MITCHELL to score.

Burnley were desperately close to a third goal when Brennan thundered a 25-yard free-kick against the underside of the Rovers crossbar five minutes from time.

The visitors could have drawn level with virtually the last kick of the game but Mitchell handled right in front of goal to let a great opportunity slip.

Burnley
A. Stevenson; K. Newton; I. Brennan; P. Noble; P. Robinson; B. Rodaway; W. Ingham; M. Smith; P. Fletcher; B. Flynn; T. Cochrane

Blackburn Rovers
P. Bradshaw; J. Curtis; J. Bailey; S. Metcalfe; G. Keeley; G. Hawkins; N. Brotherston; K. Hird; R. Mitchell; T. Parkes; D. Wagstaffe

Attendance: 8,119

Match 121
26 December 1977
Burnley 2 Blackburn Rovers 3

The match was virtually decided in the first half when Rovers, cheered on by a massive following among Burnley's biggest crowd for eighteen months, took control and scored three goals.

The third-minute goal, which set the pattern of the match, came from a low left-wing centre from Noel Brotherston, which normally would have been a defender's ball. Instead the ball fell to the unmarked David WAGSTAFFE and he forced the ball in from a narrow angle. Rovers' second goal in the 29th minute involved a good link-up down the right wing between Gordon Taylor and Kevin Hird. As Hird crossed, FEAR nipped in between Thomson and Rodaway to shoot past Stevenson. Five minutes before half-time, Rovers went 3-0 up when BROTHERSTON intercepted Hall's intended back pass, rounded Stevenson and slotted the ball into the empty net.

Within two minutes of the restart, Rovers were awarded a penalty when Hall went full length to palm away a net bound volley from Keith

Fear. The Rovers striker took the penalty-kick himself but Stevenson produced a magnificent one-handed save. Shortly afterwards, Kindon was stretchered off with a broken nose but returned to cause problems for the Blackburn defence.

However, it was Tony MORLEY who reduced the arrears with a brilliant individual goal. His speedy run from the halfway line past defenders Hird and Fazackerley was finished off with a powerful 20-yard drive wide of goalkeeper John Butcher. Six minutes from time, Noble had the ball in the Rovers net only to have the effort ruled out for handball. The Clarets persistence was rewarded a minute from time when Rovers substitute Glenn Keely panicked and handled the ball to stop a surging run from Kindon. NOBLE stepped up to slot home the perfect penalty.

Although the referee added on over seven minutes for injuries and time-wasting, time ran out for the Clarets

Burnley
A. Stevenson; K. Newton; I. Brennan; P. Noble; J. Thomson; B. Rodaway; W. Ingham (T. Cochrane); B. Hall; P. Fletcher; S. Kindon; T. Morley

Blackburn Rovers
J. Butcher; K. Hird (G. Keeley); J. Bailey; S. Metcalfe; J. Waddington; D. Fazackerley; N. Brotherston; K. Fear; D. Wagstaffe; T. Parkes; G. Taylor

Attendance: 27,427

Match 122
27 March 1978
Blackburn Rovers 0 Burnley 1

A brilliant individual goal by Burnley's Northern Ireland international winger Terry Cochrane, gave the Clarets a great start to this lively and often controversial East Lancashire Derby.

There was trouble on the terraces, eight players were booked and Rovers' Noel Brotherston was given his marching orders in a match of utmost importance to both clubs.

There was a fairly quiet opening to the match with both teams testing each other out and neither goalkeeper in the opening stages being called upon to make a save. The first spell of any real pressure came from Blackburn as Keeley had a header saved and Metcalfe chipped a shot inches too high with Stevenson beaten before Parkes missed from six yards out! Burnley's best effort in this period came from Fletcher whose header from Kindon's cross scraped Butcher's crossbar. Burnley opened the scoring in the 19th minute when COCHRANE, receiving the ball from Fletcher, set off for goal, beat Hird and hammered the ball into the net from 25 yards. Both teams were having trouble with a swirling wind and bouncing ball, which tended to make the game a little disjointed. The Clarets had a remarkable escape seconds before the interval when Hird's deep cross was headed against the post by Lewis and as Radford and Metcalfe tried to turn in the loose ball, Burnley scrambled it away with the Rovers players appealing in vain for a penalty.

Early in the second half, Stevenson palmed a Metcalfe free-kick onto the crossbar, from where it dropped behind. Burnley almost went 2-0 up when Butcher made a fine save from Brennan's 20-yard shot only for the ball to slip from his grasp. As Smith raced in to apply the finishing touch, Butcher somehow stuck out a hand to scoop the ball off the line.

Trouble broke out behind the Blackburn goal and the police moved into remove those involved. The match erupted in the 68th minute when Brotherston, who had earlier been booked for a skirmish with Brennan, was sent off after bringing down Cochrane. Burnley looked set to extend their lead in the dying moments of the game when Cochrane clean through, rounded Keeley but was foiled by a superb save by Butcher.

Blackburn Rovers
J. Butcher; K. Hird; J. Bailey; S. Metcalfe; G. Keeley; P. Round;
N. Brotherston; G. Taylor; J. Radford (D. Wagstaffe); T. Parkes; J. Lewis

Burnley
A. Stevenson; D. Scott; I. Brennan; P. Noble; J. Thomson; B. Rodaway;
T. Cochrane; W. Ingham; P. Fletcher; S. Kindon; M. Smith

Attendance: 24,379

Match 123
12 August 1978
Blackburn Rovers 1 Burnley 1

As a local derby, this Anglo-Scottish Cup game was a tame affair with hardly a foul or a wild tackle in sight all afternoon! The game was a little over a minute old when Tony Morley, replacing the injured Terry Cochrane, ran 70 yards down the touchline before pulling the ball back for Malcolm SMITH to open the scoring for the Clarets. Burnley continued to look the better side only to be surprised by a Blackburn equaliser in the ninth minute.

A neat build-up between John Bailey and Simon Garner was rounded off by Noel BROTHERSTON who toe-poked the ball into the corner of the net from 10 yards out. Garner lobbed over the bar as he beat Stevenson to a through pass whilst at the other end, Kindon hit the side-netting with Butcher beaten.

After the interval, Stevenson saved well from Garner and Metcalfe while Keeley wasted the best chance of all by heading wide from in front of an open goal. Garner came close to giving Rovers the lead when he side-footed over the top at the end of a defence-splitting four-man move.

In the last minute of the game, Burnley came close to snatching a shock winner when Morley just failed to turn in a cross from Kindon. The draw took Burnley through to the quarter-finals of the Anglo-Scottish Cup whilst the match served its purpose in providing some useful practice and in helping towards full fitness.

Blackburn Rovers
J. Butcher; K. Hird; J. Bailey; S. Metcalfe; G. Keeley; J. Waddington; N. Brotherston; M. Fowler; S. Garner; T. Parkes; J. Aston

Burnley
A. Stevenson; D. Scott; I. Brennan; P. Noble; J. Thomson; B. Rodaway; T. Morley; W. Ingham; P. Fletcher; S. Kindon; M. Smith

Attendance: 9,791

Match 124
26 December 1978
Burnley 2 Blackburn Rovers 1

A 23,133 crowd saw a lively and entertaining game of football with Rovers perhaps the better team but failing to make the most of their chances. The crowd also saw Paul FLETCHER open the scoring for the Clarets with a strange goal. He sped in to tackle John Radford near the Rovers penalty area and suddenly found himself presented with the ball. He then hit a first-time drive over the head of astonished Blackburn 'keeper John Butcher. Then Peter NOBLE made it 2-0 for Burnley just before half-time when he latched on to a pass from Billy Ingham and saw his deflected shot cannonball into the net.

Rovers did pull a goal back early in the second half when Kevin HIRD faced by three Burnley defenders, saw Alan Stevenson off his line. He then chipped in a delightful shot which entered the net off the underside of the bar. Stuart Metcalfe, who was back in action after a three-match suspension found the pace hard-going and was replaced by Fowler as Rovers caretaker-manager John Pickering sought a winning formula.

For Burnley, Welsh international Leighton James was substituted by Tony Morley after the Clarets winger found his shoulder injury troublesome. Rovers who had won just one home game in the League at this half-way point of the season, were certainly looking like relegation candidates.

Burnley
A. Stevenson; D. Scott; I. Brennan; P. Noble; J. Thomson; B. Rodaway; B. Hall; W. Ingham; P. Fletcher; S. Kindon; L. James (T. Morley)

Blackburn Rovers
J. Butcher; K. Hird; J. Bailey; S. Metcalfe (M. Fowler); G. Keeley; D. Fazackerley; N. Brotherston; J. Radford; J. Craig; P. Round; A. Birchenall

Attendance: 23,133

Match 125
14 April 1979
Blackburn Rovers 1 Burnley 2

In a match that was full of incidents, Burnley almost took the lead in the opening minute when a Kindon flick set Ingham free in the box but Parkin intercepted, putting the ball out for a corner. Jakub then went close with a 25-yard drive and Paul Fletcher shot into the side-netting with only Ramsbottom to beat. Then the Rovers 'keeper made a tremendous save from Jakub, touching another rasping drive round the post.

The Clarets were well on top in the opening stages and a strong Steve Kindon 40-yard run down the left was only stopped by a last-ditch Parkin tackle. After Garner had been penalised for a foul on Arins just outside the box, James's free-kick brought a loud penalty appeal from the Burnley fans as Parkin appeared to handle the ball in an aerial challenge with Paul Fletcher.

Rovers almost took the lead in the 16th minute when Thomson tried to head Coughlin's back pass to Stevenson. The header was short and Garner latched on to the ball but his shot was blocked by Stevenson in the Burnley goal.

Kindon, who had just been penalised for a foul on Waddington, suddenly collapsed and was stretchered off the field. Burnley played with ten men for over a quarter of an hour before Harry Potts sent on substitute Tony Morley. A minute later, Rovers took a shock lead when Bailey's cross was headed back to GARNER who made no mistake from close in. The home side almost extended their lead when McKenzie's shot on the turn brought a magnificent reflex save out of Stevenson.

Just ten seconds into the second half, a terrible mistake by Rovers centre-half John Waddington let in MORLEY for the equaliser. A minute later, another skip let in Morley again but his shot shaved the post with Ramsbottom scrambling to recover. Brotherston then miskicked in front of a gaping Burnley goal and as the ball ran to Fowler, his shot was saved by Stevenson at the second attempt. Burnley took the lead in the 71st minute, slightly against the run of play when Noble's flick landed in the path of Brian HALL who gave Ramsbottom no chance from close in.

Sadly, the game was marred by a lot of trouble on the terraces at the Darwen End, with police constantly escorting fans out.

Blackburn Rovers
N. Ramsbottom; M. Rathbone; J. Bailey; R. Coughlin; T. Parkin; J. Waddington; N. Brotherston; M. Fowler; S. Garner; P. Round; D. McKenzie

Burnley
A. Stevenson; A. Arins; J. Jakub; P. Noble; J. Thomson; B. Rodaway; B. Hall; W. Ingham; P. Fletcher; S. Kindon (T. Morley); L. James

Attendance: 14,761

Match 126
4 August 1979
Blackburn Rovers 2 Burnley 2

All eyes were on Burnley's record signing Martin Dobson, back in the Turf Moor fold after five years with Everton. The England international didn't disappoint – he was the dominant figure, hungry for the ball and prompting many of the Clarets' best moves.

The visitors got the perfect start when Peter Noble headed on a long throw from Derek Scott in the first minute and Steve KINDON nipped in to steer his shot wide of Jim Arnold. Kindon came close to adding to his tally, sending a couple of shots marginally off target. The half-time whistle sounded with neither goalkeeper having made a noteworthy save.

Within a minute of the restart, Rovers had equalised when Northern Ireland international winger Noel BROTHERSTON was put clear by Joe Craig. He stepped inside two defenders before firing a left foot shot into the far top corner. Paul Fletcher then brought the save of the match out of Jim Arnold before at the other end, Joe Jakub scrambled Craig's shot off the line.

Burnley went ahead in the 68th minute when Stuart METCALFE racing back to cover, got his head to a Kindon cross and sent it looping wide of Arnold for an own-goal!

Rovers equalised 11 minutes from time when CRAIG headed home Kendall's free-kick past a flat-footed Stevenson in the Burnley goal.

Blackburn Rovers
J. Arnold; P. Round; B. Morley; H. Kendall; G. Keeley; D. Fazackerley; N. Brotherston; D. McKenzie; J. Craig; S. Metcalfe; T. Parkes

Burnley
A. Stevenson; D. Scott; J. Jakub; P. Noble; J. Thomson; B. Rodaway; W. Ingham; M. Dobson; P. Fletcher; S. Kindon; L. James

Attendance: 7,749

Match 127
27 December 1982
Burnley 0 Blackburn Rovers 1

One lethal moment of finishing power from Blackburn Rover's leading scorer, Simon Garner, was enough to settle the East Lancashire Derby.

The goal after 32 minutes was the highlight of an otherwise dull first half in which scoring chances were at a premium. A long free-kick by Derek Fazackerley saw Norman Bell beat Clarets debutant Mike Walsh in the air and GARNER fastening on to the ball, blasted home past O'Rourke from point-blank range. The goal gave Rovers much more confidence, especially to the defence, which went on to keep three clean sheets in a row.

The game was certainly not one for the purists. Played at a frenetic pace in blustery, showery conditions, the skill factor was submerged in the cut and thrust of a typical derby match.

The first half was a fairly nondescript affair with Burnley's brightest spell being a series of corners midway through the opening period. The outcome might have been different if Steve Taylor's shot in the 13th minute had counted but his 'goal' was disallowed for pushing on David Mail. Both the referee and linesman were in accord which was not the case on the hour-mark when David Hamilton thought he had extended

Rovers' lead when he headed home a cross from Randell. This time, referee Alex Hamill gave offside though the linesman kept his flag down!

Burnley's reserve 'keeper Billy O'Rourke gave an outstanding display. Despite receiving a cut head in a 7th-minute clash with Garner and later needing four stitches, O'Rourke never faltered and twice foiled Garner with fine saves.

The Clarets should have equalised in the 72nd minute but Billy Hamilton headed straight at Terry Gennoe while Steve Taylor was put clean through only to be thwarted when the Rovers 'keeper dived at his feet. With that chance went Burnley's hopes of saving a point. Garner almost made it 2-0 in the dying minutes but his lob after Dobson had misjudged a long punt downfield from Gennoe, landed on the roof of the net!

Burnley
W. O'Rourke; B. Laws; D. Holt; T. Cassidy; M. Phelan; B. Flynn; M. Dobson; T. Steven; B. Hamilton; S. Taylor; M. Walsh

Blackburn Rovers
T. Gennoe; J. Branagan; M. Rathbone; C. Randell; D. Mail; D. Fazackerley; I. Miller; D. Hamilton; N. Bell; S. Garner; N. Brotherston

Attendance: 20,439

Match 128
4 April 1983
Blackburn Rovers 2 Burnley 1

The one thing that this Easter Derby will not be remembered for is the standard of football – it was so instantly forgettable! Rovers fans at least had the satisfaction of a 'double' and their first home league win over Burnley for 21 years. But it was a black day all round for the game with the unprecedented sight of an Ewood match being held up for 16 minutes in the second half because of crowd violence on the Darwen End terracing. It produced some of the most sickening scenes ever witnessed on a football ground, which prior to the stoppage, smoke bombs and a whisky bottle had been thrown on to the pitch.

Rovers could have been in front in the 11th minute when Alan Stevenson fumbled a Garner cross but David Hamilton's shot hit the underside of the bar. A minute later, Rovers lost Ian Miller who had to limp off with a knee injury. Burnley's only first half effort of note was a

30-yard drive from Kevin Young, which grazed the outside of Gennoe's right-hand post.

The game itself was desperately poor until Simon GARNER proved himself the coolest man on the ground by scoring from a controversial twice-taken penalty after 59 minutes to inject some badly needed life into the proceedings. Rovers could have made it safe.

After the mayhem on the terraces, GARNER was spot-on again in the 76th minute after Flynn was adjudged to have pushed Hamilton as Stevenson dived at his feet. Rovers could have made it safe but for an incredible double miss by Norman Bell, allied to some goal-line heroics from Brian Flynn while at the other end, Trevor Steven was only inches away from connecting with a header.

With six minutes remaining, Derek SCOTT managed to halve the arrears but time ran out for the Clarets as they went in search of an equaliser.

Blackburn Rovers
T. Gennoe; J. Branagan; M. Rathbone; C. Randell; D. Mail; D. Fazackerley; I. Miller (N. Bell); D. Hamilton; J. Lowey; S. Garner; N. Brotherston

Burnley
A. Stevenson; B. Laws; W. Donnachie; M. Phelan; M. Dobson; B. Flynn; D. Scott; T. Steven; B. Hamilton; S. Taylor; K. Young

Attendance: 13,434

Match 129
16 August 1983
Burnley 1 Blackburn Rovers 1

Blackburn Rovers took the lead after just two minutes of this Lancashire Manx Cup clash when Clarets 'keeper Roger Hansbury could only parry a fiercely struck free-kick from Randell and Michael Phelan had to clear for a corner before Simon Garner could strike. But the danger wasn't over and, after Hansbury had failed to cut out Randell's corner, GARNER forced the ball in at the far post.

Right-winger Ian Miller almost added another four minutes later but he floated a 20-yard shot over Hansbury and onto the roof of the net. At the other end, Kevin Reeves had a header and a shot blocked at close-range and then tricked his way into the penalty area before firing in a left-foot shot which O'Keefe saved with his knees. Just before half-time,

Garner limped off with a leg injury, leaving Rovers with a punchless attack.

As the game wore on, the Clarets took command, forcing Rovers to defend in numbers. Reeves had a 51st-minute volley saved by O'Keefe whilst Donnachie and Gallagher were booked as Burnley's frustration at failing to equalise, grew.

With time running out, Burnley were awarded a free-kick 25 yards out after Keeley had brought down Phelan. SCOTT's shot was deflected off the head of Randell and over O'Keefe and into the net for the equaliser.

A booking for Branagan. for kicking the ball away at a free-kick, was the only other noteworthy incident as the match petered out to a tame conclusion.

Burnley
R. Hansbury; B. Laws; W. Donnachie; M. Phelan; K. Gallagher; B. Flynn; D. Scott; K. Reeves; B. Hamilton; G. Gow; T. Hutchison

Blackburn Rovers
V. O'Keefe; J. Branagan; M. Rathbone; C. Randell; G. Keeley; D. Fazackerley; I. Miller; J. Lowey; N. Bell; S. Garner (C. Thompson); D. Hamilton

Attendance: 6,488

Match 130
13 August 1985
Blackburn Rovers 1 Burnley 0

A superbly taken goal by Rovers striker Simon Garner, 12 minutes from the end, pipped the Clarets in this highly entertaining Lancashire Manx Cup Final at Ewood Park.

The first half belonged to the visitors, who though a Fourth Division side, had enough chances to have humiliated the Rovers. Wayne Biggins headed wide of Gennoe's right-hand post when normally he would have expected to hit the target. Kevin Hird, who was returning to the Ewood Park scene where he began his career brought a fine save out of Gennoe and then he put Taylor clean through but the Burnley centre-forward shot straight at the Rovers 'keeper.

It was a different story in the second half with Clarets 'keeper Joe Neenan forced to save low to his right in the opening minutes to turn Garner's shot round the post. The big Burnley 'keeper seemed unbeatable but in the 88th minute, GARNER, receiving the ball from Jimmy

Quinn, cut inside Palmer before cracking the ball over the head of the Burnley 'keeper and into the roof of the net.

With the Isle of Man trophy already on the Ewood sideboard and now this to keep it company, Rovers completed their eighth game in 16 days!

Blackburn Rovers
T. Gennoe; D. Hamilton; M. Rathbone; S. Barker; G. Keeley; D. Mail; I. Miller; J. Lowey; J. Quinn; S. Garner; N. Brotherston

Burnley
J. Neenan; G. Palmer; P. Hampton; J. Heggarty; V. Overson; R. Deakin; N. Grewcock; P. Malley; S. Taylor: W. Biggins; K. Hird

Attendance: 6,017

Match 131
4 August 1987
Burnley 2 Blackburn Rovers 1

Not only did Burnley beat Rovers, who were two divisions higher but did so after coming from a goal behind after only 16 minutes.

After both sides had seen goals turned down – Howard Gayle for Rovers because Pearce was fouled and Neil Grewcock for Burnley because he was offside – Rovers took the lead when Colin Hendry sent the ball through the middle for CURRY to beat Pearce.

Both sides were denied what seemed blatant penalties – Rovers after Ray Deakin had made a desperate tackle on Gayle and the Clarets after John Millar had upended George Oghani.

The Clarets levelled the scores in the 23rd minute when Simon Barker miscued a pass, sending the ball to Paul COMSTIVE who netted with a left-foot shot across goalkeeper Terry Gennoe.

Rovers attacked furiously and Farrell cleared off the line from Curry before Pearce turned over a Nicky Reid piledriver. The Burnley 'keeper then made an even better save from an attempted point-blank clearance from Oghani.

Just before half-time, Grewcock raced away, rounded David Mail and pulled the ball back for Ian BRITTON to score from ten yards out.

The second half didn't measure up to the first and with play getting a little heated, a number of players on both sides were booked. Rovers' John Millar who received a yellow card for blatant obstruction of Comstive, was lucky not to be sent off when he and some of his colleagues, literally trampled on Grewcock in a last-minute explosion by the corner flag.

Burnley
G. Pearce; P. Leebrook; S. McGrory; P. Daniel; S. Gardner; R. Deakin; N. Grewcock; A. Farrell; G. Oghani; P. Comstive; I. Britton (A. Hoskin)

Blackburn Rovers
T. Gennoe; C. Price (C. Sulley); J. Millar; S. Barker; K. Hill; D. Mail (M. Patterson); H. Gayle; N. Reid; C. Hendry; S. Curry; S. Sellars

Attendance: 2,501

Match 132
9 August 1988
Burnley 1 Blackburn Rovers 3

Rovers took the lead in this Manx Cup tie in the 44th minute with one of the most controversial goals in the fixture's history. Scott Sellars on the right sent over a corner which was dropping before Andy Kennedy with his hands, helped the ball gain height again before dropping at the feet of Ian MILLER who drove the ball first time from 20 yards into the net. Referee Neil Midgely turned down Burnley's protests, whilst the incident was the half-time talking point – with some Rovers players watching the game from the stand, agreeing that Kennedy had got away with it!

Early in the second half, midfielder Tony FINNIGAN extended Rovers' lead with a cracking shot from 25 yards and then KENNEDY curled in a third goal for the visitors in the 69th minute. The Rovers striker almost got another a minute later, as his header went only inches over the angle of the goal.

On 82 minutes, Burnley were awarded a penalty when George Oghani was brought down by Rovers 'keeper Collier as he was going round him. Paul COMSTIVE's left-foot shot sent the Rovers 'keeper the wrong way but to be fair it was only in the last quarter-of-an-hour or so that the Clarets began to go forward with some purpose.

Burnley
D. Williams; P. Daniel (I. Britton); R. Deakin; A. Farrell; S. Davis; S. Gardner; G. Rowell; G. Oghani; B. O'Connell; P. Comstive; P. Atkinson

Blackburn Rovers
D. Collier; M. Atkins; J. Millar; A. Finnigan; C. Hendry; K. Hill; I. Miller (A. Diamond); A. Ainscow; A. Kennedy; S. Garner; S. Sellars (L. Johnrose)

Attendance: 7,506

Match 133
8 August 1989
Burnley 0 Blackburn Rovers 2

The highlights of a splendid see-saw first half were two brilliant saves by the respective goalkeepers, Burnley's Chris Pearce and Rovers' Terry Gennoe.

It was Gennoe's turn first, when after 23 minutes, Clarets striker Brendan O'Connell lashed in a drive from fully 25 yards which flew towards the top corner of the Rovers goal, only for Gennoe to hurl himself to his left and turn the ball behind for a corner. Within five minutes, Burnley skipper Ray Deakin misdirected a header straight to Tony Finnigan but with only Pearce to beat, he shot wide of the goal. Just before half-time a mix-up between Deakin and White on the halfway line, allowed Hendry to send Garner away. The Rovers striker took the ball on before crossing hard and low for Scott SELLARS to tap in.

The second half was only three minutes old when John Millar produced a defence-splitting pass from the halfway line to send STAPLETON clear; his decisive finish gave the advancing Pearce no chance at all.

It could have signalled the start of a goal rush by the visitors but to their credit, Burnley didn't fold up and posed Rovers' strong defence one or two anxious moments before the end.

Burnley
G. Pearce; I. Measham (P. Comstive); J. Jakub; R. Deakin; M. Monington; J. Harris; N. Grewcock; P. Mumby; B. O'Connell; A. Farrell; W. White (G. Rowell)

Blackburn Rovers
T. Gennoe; M. Atkins; A. Dawson; A. Finnigan; C. Hendry; K. Hill; H. Gayle; J. Miller; F. Stapleton; S. Garner; S. Sellars

Attendance: 9,007

Match 134
17 December 2000
Burnley 0 Blackburn Rovers 2

Much had been made in the build-up to this, the first Football League meeting between the clubs in 17 years and it was clear that the occasion got to Burnley players and fans alike. Whilst Rovers have savoured the

Premiership highs, Claret fans have had to watch their team toil in the depths of the League's basement.

Early in the game, Jason McAteer made a miraculous saving interception after a fine turn and cross by Ian Moore, while Andy Payton had a shot well saved by Rovers 'keeper Brad Friedel. Man-of-the-Match McATEER headed the opening goal two minutes into time added on at the end of the first half when the Burnley defence dithered in trying to clear Stig Bjornebye's long throw-in. Rovers should have wrapped the game up a minute into the second half. Again Bjornebye's throw completely bamboozled Burnley's defenders, allowing McAteer time and space to turn and shoot. His shot hit the foot of the post but Hughes then somehow managed to spoon his effort over the unguarded goal.

In the 77th minute, Burnley's Kevin Ball was sent off for a thunderous lunge on Rovers' David Dunn. It was a shocking challenge and ignited an already highly-charged atmosphere. On at least two occasions, several players became involved in minor scuffles off the ball. As so often happens, Ball's dismissal only served to spur on the Clarets and their ten men redoubled their efforts to find a way back into an intriguing contest. Ian Moore did find the back of the net but the referee adjudged that the Burnley striker had fouled Brad Friedel in the process.

However, Rovers' recent signing from Sheffield United, Marcus BENT, wrapped up the points with another close-range header as Nik Michopolous parried a drive from substitute Alan Mahon who was making his debut for Blackburn after arriving on loan from Sporting Lisbon.

To sum up, Rovers had the touch of class to complement their necessary steel as they gave Burnley a lesson in keeping one's nerve at a hate-filled Turf Moor!

Burnley
N. Michopolous; M. Thomas; I. Cox; S. Davis; P. Cook (L. Johnrose); K. Ball; G. Branch (B. Maylett); A. Payton; M. Mellon (J. Mullen); I. Moore; P. Weller

Blackburn Rovers
B. Freidel; J. Curtis; J. McAteer; S. Bjornebye; G. Flitcroft; D. Dunn; M. Hughes (M. Jansen); D. Duff (A. Mahon); M. Bent; M. Taylor; H. Berg

Attendance: 21,369

Match 135
1 April 2001
Blackburn Rovers 5 Burnley 0

Burnley suffered their heaviest League defeat at the hands of Blackburn Rovers for 71 years and if the home side had taken all their chances, they would easily have eclipsed their record win over the Clarets – a 7-1 victory in 1888.

On a day of tight security inside and outside the ground, Steve Davis almost put through his own goal after eight minutes when he turned a low cross from David Dunn against his own bar. Five minutes later, Rovers opened the scoring when defender Craig SHORT stuck out his foot to deflect a low drive from Dunn into the net for his first goal in five years. After 18 minutes, Short popped up wide on the left to create Rovers' second goal. As he tried to pick out a team-mate with a cross, the ball hit the unfortunate DAVIS and rolled over the line. There was brief hope for Burnley when Ian Moore smashed home a shot after 36 minutes but the referee ruled offside.

Graeme Souness' side went on to help themselves to three more goals in the second half, with Matt Jansen netting two of them. JANSEN claimed his first from a few yards out after 56 minutes following a powerful run and cross by Marcus Bent. JANSEN's second came after 71 minutes, following a fine run by Alan Mahon. Rovers substitute Craig HIGNETT wrapped it up in the 84th minute with a low drive from the edge of the penalty area.

Rovers who needed a four-goal winning margin to go above their other neighbours Bolton Wanderers into second place on goal difference, did so in style – their fans celebrating the completion of a double on the resumption of this league fixture after a 17-year absence.

Blackburn Rovers

B. Freidel; J. Curtis; J. McAteer (C. Hignett); C. Short; G. Flitcroft; D. Dunn; D. Duff (S. Bjornebye); M. Jansen; M. Bent; H. Berg (M. Hughes); A. Mahon

Burnley

N. Michopolous; M. Thomas; S. Davis; G. Little; P. Cook; M. Taylor; G. Branch (P. Smith); I. Moore (G. Armstrong); P. Weller; K. Ball (A. Payton); I. Cox

Attendance: 22,442

Star Players

Jimmy Adamson (Burnley)

Within three years of making his debut, Jimmy Adamson had won England 'B' honours when he played in the first-ever meeting with Scotland 'B' at Edinburgh. He also represented the Football League and although a full international cap eluded him, success at Turf Moor did not. He skippered the Clarets to the League Championship in 1959-60 and two years later, led Burnley to the FA Cup Final where despite losing to Spurs, he was named Footballer of the Year. Also in 1962, he was a member of England's World Cup squad in Chile, later turning down the chance of managing his country! After playing the last of his 486 games, he became coach at Turf Moor, being appointed manager in 1970. He led the Clarets to the Second Division Championship and to sixth place in the top flight. He later managed Sunderland and Leeds United before ending his involvement with the game.

John Angus (Burnley)

In a career that spanned three decades, John Angus won a League Championship medal in 1959-60 and an FA Cup runners-up medal in 1962. Unfortunate to be around at the same time as Blackpool's Jimmy Armfield, he won only one full cap, though he had won seven Under-23 caps and represented the Football League.

One of the best right-backs in the top flight, he went on to appear in 521 League and Cup games for the Clarets, scoring four goals. Two of his strikes came in the same match in October 1964 when Burnley went down 3-2 to Arsenal. His playing days over, he severed all connections with the game and went to live and work in Northumberland.

Adam Blacklaw (Blackburn Rovers and Burnley)

Following the injury Colin McDonald sustained while playing for the Football League, Adam Blacklaw made the goalkeeping position his own. His performances in Burnley's League Championship winning season of 1959-60 leading to him making two appearances for the Scotland Under-23 side. Ever-present in seasons 1961-62, 1962-63 and 1963-64, he appeared in 172 consecutive league games and won three full caps for his country. After his place came under threat from Harry Thomson, Blacklaw, who had played in 383 League and Cup games for the Clarets, joined Blackburn Rovers.

He spent three seasons at Ewood Park before ending his league career with Blackpool. He later played non-League football for Great Harwood before managing Clitheroe.

Tommy Boyle (Burnley)

Tommy Boyle began his career with his local club, Barnsley, leading them to the 1910 FA Cup Final against Newcastle before Burnley splashed out a club record fee of £1,150 to bring him to Turf Moor. Appointed captain, he led the Clarets to promotion to the First Division in 1912-13 and the following season became the only Burnley skipper to lift the FA Cup when it was presented to him by King George V following the Clarets' 1-0 victory over Liverpool. Despite suffering serious injuries during the First World War, the England international defender lined-up for Burnley after the hostilities and in 1920-21 captained the club to the League Championship as they went a record 30 games without defeat. He went on to score 43 goals in 236 games before becoming player-coach at Wrexham.

Tom Brandon (Blackburn Rovers)

Full-back Tom Brandon joined Rovers from St Mirren in 1889 but having won an FA Cup winners' medal in 1891, he crossed the Pennines to play for Sheffield Wednesday. He captained the side into the Football League but within a year, he was back at Ewood Park. The tough-tackling defender, who won full international honours for Scotland, also appeared for the Football League whilst with Rovers. During his final years with the club he was also a landlord in the town but in 1900 after scoring two goals in 243 League and Cup appearances, he returned north of the border to end his playing career with his first club, St Mirren.

Jack Bruton (Blackburn Rovers and Burnley)

A former pit lad, Jack Bruton played for Horwich RMI and Wigan Borough before joining Burnley. While with the Clarets, he represented the Football League and made three appearances for England. After scoring 40 goals in 168 games, he left Turf Moor to join Blackburn Rovers for a fee of £6,500.

An extremely skilful forward, a maker as well as a scorer of goals, Bruton missed very few games in nine seasons with the club, netting 115 goals in 344 games. On hanging up his boots, he became the club's assistant-trainer and secretary before becoming assistant-manager. On Will Scott's departure, he took over the reins but after the club failed to win promotion, he was released, though the parting of the ways was somewhat bitter. He later managed Bournemouth before returning to Ewood Park as the club's scout.

Len Butt (Blackburn Rovers)

Joining Stockport County from Wilmslow Albion, Len Butt found it difficult to make an impact in League football and in 1932 moved back into non-League with Macclesfield. Huddersfield Town gave him the chance to resurrect his league career and after a series of impressive displays, he joined Blackburn Rovers in 1937.

Able to create and score goals, Butt was a regular member of Rovers' Second Division Championship winning team of 1938-39 and appeared for the Ewood Park club in the 1940 War Cup Final. A knee injury sustained during the war years took the edge off his game and in January 1947 after scoring 48 goals in 117 League and Cup games, he was transferred to York City later ending his career with Mansfield Town.

Ronnie Clayton (Blackburn Rovers)

Ronnie Clayton had natural leadership qualities which showed early in his career. In September 1955 he won his first Under-23 cap and a month later he appeared for the England 'B' team. In November of that year, he completed the international sequence when he won the first of 35 caps for the full England team.

A tremendous driving force in Blackburn's promotion to the First Division in 1957-58, he appeared in the final stages of the 1958 World Cup and led Rovers to the FA Cup Final in 1960. An energetic wing-half, strong in the tackle and a brilliant timer of the ball in the air, he went on to score 16 goals in 665 League and Cup games for Rovers before becoming player-manager of Morecambe. Without doubt, one of the greatest players ever to wear the Rovers colours.

John Connelly (Blackburn Rovers and Burnley)

One of the top-scoring wingmen in the game throughout the late fifties and early sixties, John Connelly was a member of Burnley's Championship-winning side of 1959-60, scoring 20 goals in 34 games. His form that season led to him winning the first of 20 full caps for England, including an appearance against Uruguay

in the 1966 World Cup Finals. Connelly netted two hat-tricks for the Clarets, the last against Manchester United whom he later joined for 60,000 in April 1964, having scored 105 goals in 265 games for the Turf Moor club. In his first season at old Trafford, he helped the Reds win the League Championship but a year later he left to play for Blackburn

Rovers. He continued to find the net, scoring 36 goals in 149 games before ending his first-class career with Bury.

Bob Crompton (Blackburn Rovers)

Bob Crompton won most of the honours which the game had to offer. He was club captain of two championship-winning sides, an international for over ten years and captain of England. He had natural leadership qualities and as captain, ensured that all the Rovers team followed his own high standards of fair play. Crompton made 576 League and Cup appearances for Rovers and though he played a couple of games in 1919-20, the First World War effectively ended his playing career.

In 1926, he was appointed Blackburn manager, a popular choice with the fans, who still regarded him as the greatest player the club had produced. He led Rovers to victory in the 1928 FA Cup Final and though he lost his job in 1931, he returned seven years later and in 1938-39 took the club into the First Division as champions of Division Two. He took Rovers to the 1940 War Cup Final but in March 1941, the greatest figure in the club's history, collapsed and died.

Walter Crook (Blackburn Rovers)

Though he made his Rovers debut in 1932 when just a few weeks short of his 20th birthday, it was the 1934-35 season before he established himself in the Blackburn side. Able to play on either flank, the aggressive full-back became club captain and led the team to the Second Division Championship in 1938-39. Although he was a member of the Rovers side that won the 1940 War Cup Final, military service restricted his wartime appearances. On his return to Ewood Park after the hostilities, he clashed with new manager Eddie Hapgood and after scoring two goals in 237 League and Cup games, he joined Bolton Wanderers. Sadly injuries forced him into early retirement and after coaching Ajax of Amsterdam, he managed Accrington Stanley, later ending his involvement with the game after 18 years as Preston North End's trainer.

Jerry Dawson (Burnley)

The holder of the club record for the greatest number of appearances, Jerry Dawson was Burnley's first-choice goalkeeper for 15 seasons either side of the First World War. In 1910, he represented the Football League against the Scottish League at Ewood Park and again the following year at Ibrox Park. In 1912-13 he helped the club win promotion to the First Division and reach the FA Cup semi-finals but was injured the following season after helping the Clarets win through to the FA Cup Final.

Dawson was still in goal when the club won the League Championship for the first time in their history in 1920-21, his form leading to him winning two full caps for his country. Dawson was 40 years 282 days old when he made the last of his 569 League and Cup appearances for Burnley against Liverpool on Christmas Day 1928.

Percy Dawson (Blackburn Rovers)

Percy Dawson made his name north of the border with Heart of Midlothian before Rovers paid £2,500 for his services in 1914. After helping the club win the League Championship, Dawson scored 20 goals in 28 games in 1914-15 as Rovers made an unsuccessful attempt to retain their Championship. Included in this total were four of Rovers' goals in a 6-0 thrashing of Burnley at Ewood Park. When League football resumed after the First World War, Dawson was one of the few experienced players left at the club. Though he strove hard to hold the front line together, he was no longer the player he was and in 1923 after scoring 73 goals in 151 League and Cup games, he hung up his boots.

Peter Dobing (Blackburn Rovers)

Son of a former Salford Rugby League player, Peter Dobing was the club's leading scorer when they won promotion to the First Division in 1957-58 with 20 goals in 34 games including four in a 5-0 defeat of Bristol City. Dobing headed Rovers' scoring charts again in 1958-59 with 24 goals in the top flight including a hat-trick in a 4-2 win over Arsenal. Leading scorer for the next two seasons, he netted five in Rovers' run to the FA Cup Final in 1960 and though he won England honours at Under-23 level and represented the Football League, he was unable to break into the full England side. He had scored 104 goals in 205 games when he left to join Manchester City. Unable to settle at Maine Road, he signed for Stoke, leading them to victory in the 1972 League Cup Final.

Bryan Douglas (Blackburn Rovers)

In his early days at Ewood Park, Bryan Douglas was often criticised for being over-elaborate and too selfish. Deceptively frail-looking, he was later to confound those critics and become one of England's greatest post-war footballers, scoring 11 goals in 36 appearances for his country. Rovers preferred to use him as a scheming inside-forward and for more than a decade, he made a succession of forwards into frequent goalscorers. Douglas was a member of the Blackburn side that reached the FA Cup Final in 1960 and played in all four of England's games in the 1962 World Cup Finals in Chile. Sadly his final years at Ewood Park were dogged by injury and in 1969 after scoring 111 goals in 503 games, he left Rovers to spend a couple of seasons playing non-League football with Great Harwood.

John Forbes (Blackburn Rovers)

A leading figure in the history of Blackburn Rovers, John Forbes played his early football with Vale of Leven, for whom he appeared in two Scottish Cup Finals. In November 1889, Forbes moved to Blackburn Rovers and within a short time, had become a member of the club's committee. The quick-tackling full-back led Rovers to victories in the 1890 and 1891 FA Cup Finals, though sadly after the second success, a 3-1 win over Notts County, ill-health forced him into premature retirement. On hanging up his boots, Forbes set up a gentlemen's outfitters and became a member of the board, a position he held until his death in 1928.

Simon Garner (Blackburn Rovers)

Simon Garner's pace and power made him a handful for most Second Division defences and on 10 September 1983, he scored all five goals as Rovers beat Derby County 5-1. During the 1980s, Garner was recognised as one of the deadliest marksmen outside of the top flight. He established a goalscoring record for the Rovers in 1988-89, taking his aggregate total to 144 goals to overhaul the record set by Tommy Briggs of 140 league goals between 1952 and 1958. The record came in the match against Manchester City when he netted a hat-trick in a 4-0 win. Garner, who scored 192 goals in 565 games, later helped West Bromwich Albion win promotion to the top flight before ending his league career with Wycombe Wanderers.

Ted Harper (Blackburn Rovers)

Ted Harper joined Blackburn Rovers from non-League Shepey United and in 1923-24 his first season with the club, he scored 18 goals, the highest tally for the Ewood Park club since the First World War. In 1925-26, Harper scored 43 league goals in 37 games including a hat-trick in a 3-1 win over the Clarets at Turf Moor – a record which has remained intact. His goalscoring talents led to him winning full international honours and shortly afterwards he left Rovers to play for Sheffield Wednesday. A year later he joined Tottenham Hotspur before returning north to play for Preston North End. In 1934, he rejoined Rovers for a second spell, taking his tally of goals to 122 in 177 games before hanging up his boots.

Harry Healless (Blackburn Rovers)

Capable of playing in any of the half-back positions, Harry Healless' first appearances for Blackburn Rovers were in the forward line. A tireless worker, strong in the tackle and good in the air, coupled with his ability to motivate players, made him an ideal choice for captaincy. An England international, his greatest moment came when he held the FA Cup aloft in 1928 after Rovers had beaten Huddersfield Town 3-1 in the final. Healless went on to score 13 goals in 396 League and Cup games, making his last appearance just days before his 40th birthday. After a spell coaching Dutch side Almelo, he returned to Ewood Park in a similar capacity, departing upon the appointment of Johnny Carey.

Jimmy Hill (Burnley)

Jimmy Hill joined the Clarets from St Mirren in December 1889. When he arrived at Turf Moor, Burnley were lying bottom of the League and it was his partnership with Claude Lambie that helped them win four of their last five games and so finish in 11th place. Hill was the club's first real consistent goalscorer with his best season being 1893-94, when he netted 11 goals in 25 games. His only hat-trick for the Clarets came two seasons later in a 4-3 win at Bury. He had scored 41 goals in 162 games for Burnley when in January 1897 he left to play for Stoke.

After one-and-a-half seasons he left the Victoria Ground, being tempted to join New Brighton Tower who were offering much higher money!

Jack Hillman (Burnley)

Second only to the Sheffield United 'keeper Billy Foulke in stature, Jack Hillman stood over 6ft and weighed 16 stone. After four seasons in the Burnley side, he joined Everton before signing for Dundee. His stay north of the border was brief and, in March 1898, he returned to Turf Moor. After making his England debut in a 13-2 defeat of Ireland, he was banned for the entire 1900-01 season following an attempt to bribe Nottingham Forest players to 'throw' the last game of the 1899-1900 season and so enable Burnley to avoid relegation to the Second Division. He returned the following season but after 188 appearances, he joined Manchester City, helping them win the Second Division Championship and the FA Cup before becoming Burnley's trainer.

Bob Kelly (Burnley)

Having joined the Clarets from St Helens Town prior to the First World War, Bob Kelly was at his best in 1919-20, helping the club finish runners-up in the First Division and winning the first of 14 full caps for England when he scored in a 5-4 win over Scotland. In 1920-21, he was an influential member of Burnley's League Championship winning side, scoring 20 goals in 37 games including four in a 7-1 defeat of Oldham Athletic. He went on to score 97 goals in 299 League and Cup games before leaving Turf Moor in December 1925 to join Sunderland. Just over a year later he moved to Huddersfield Town, making over 200 appearances for the Terriers before spells with Preston North End and Carlisle United. He later managed Stockport County to the Third Division title in 1936-37.

Sandy Lang (Burnley)

Able to play on either flank, Paisley-born full-back Sandy Lang joined Burnley from Padiham in 1885. When League football came to Turf Moor, Lang was the club's captain, the tough-tackling defender being the first Clarets player to complete 100 games for the club. Lang was also the first Burnley player to score from the penalty-spot when he converted his kick in the 3-2 win over West Bromwich Albion in November 1891. Lang went on to appear in 134 League and Cup games before leaving to become a publican in the town. He later returned to the game, helping Nelson win the Lancashire League before at the age of only 37, he sustained fatal injuries in an accident at home.

Mick McGrath (Blackburn Rovers)

Mick McGrath established himself in the Rovers side in 1957-58, playing in every game of the club's promotion-winning season. A hard-tackling wing-half who appeared for the Football League, McGrath was also a regular in the Republic of Ireland side, making 18 appearances for his country whilst with Rovers. He had the misfortune to put through his own goal to open the scoring for Wolves in the 1960 FA Cup Final as Rovers went down 3-0. A perfect clubman, he retained his place in the side until March 1966 when after scoring 12 goals in 312 games, he joined Bradford Park Avenue. He later played non-League football for Bangor City before returning to Ewood Park to help out with Rovers' youth teams.

Jimmy McIlroy (Burnley)

Joining the Clarets from Glentoran, Jimmy McIlroy became recognised as one of the most accomplished inside-forwards of the post-war era. Capped 55 times by Northern Ireland, he and Danny Blanchflower masterminded the country to their greatest heights in the 1958 World

Cup when they reached the quarter-finals. McIlroy played a major role in Burnley's Championship triumph of 1959-60 and two years later picked up an FA Cup finalists medal but in March 1963 after scoring 131 goals in 497 games, he joined Stoke City for £25,000. He made an immediate impact at the Victoria Ground, helping the Potters win the Second Division title. After finishing his career with Oldham Athletic, he spent 18 days in charge of Bolton Wanderers before becoming a much respected sports journalist.

John McIntyre (Blackburn Rovers)

After playing his early football with Partick Thistle, John McIntyre came south of the border to play for Fulham and later Sheffield Wednesday. He arrived at Ewood Park in January 1922, quickly settling into the Rovers side. Later that year, he scored four goals in five minutes in Rovers 5-1 win over Everton. Before being given an extended run on the left-wing, he netted a hat-trick in Rovers 5-3 East Lancashire Derby victory at Turf Moor in September 1924. With age beginning to tell, he was converted into a wing-half, taking his total of League and Cup appearances in which he scored 39 goals to 194 before leaving to end his career with Blackpool.

Tom McLintock (Burnley)

After impressing in Scottish junior football, Tom McLintock joined Clyde before being transferred to Kilmarnock. He signed for Burnley in the summer of 1892, though he had to wait a couple of seasons before establishing himself in the Clarets' side. In 1897-98 he won a Second Division Championship medal with the Clarets and was unlucky not to win full international honours for Scotland. On losing his left-back position to George Lockhart, he showed his versatility by appearing in a number of different positions. On 13 April 1901, whilst playing on the left-wing, he scored all four goals in a 4-0 defeat of Blackpool. McLintock had scored 14 goals in 254 games before returning north of the border to rejoin Kilmarnock.

Harold Mather (Burnley)

Harold Mather joined Burnley in 1938 and though he appeared in 132 wartime games, he had to wait for the opening game of the 1946-47 season against Coventry City before making his league debut. That season, Mather was ever-present as the Clarets won promotion to the top flight and reached the FA Cup Final. Mather missed very few games over the next seven seasons, making the last of his 329 appearances against

Leicester City in September 1954. On leaving Turf Moor, he became player-coach at Nelson before being appointed coach at Hull City. He then held a number of coaching posts in South Africa, before returning to the North-West as player-manager of Nelson.

Brian Miller (Burnley)

When the Clarets won the League Championship in 1959-60, Brian Miller was ever-present, his form earning him selection for the England Under-23 side. After another successful season in 1960-61 Miller won his only full England cap against Austria in Vienna but was played out of position in a match England lost 3-1. Miller went on to score 37 goals in 455 games for Burnley with two of his goals coming in the two-legged European Fairs match against Eintrackt Frankfurt. Only four days after this tie, he damaged his knee in a game at Aston Villa and was forced to retire. After a spell on the coaching staff, he replaced Harry Potts as manager, leading the club to the Third Division title. Sacked in January 1983, he returned as manager in the summer of 1986 but later lost his position to Frank Casper.

Tom Nicol (Blackburn Rovers and Burnley)

Tom Nicol netted a hat-trick on his Burnley debut as the Clarets beat Preston North End 6-1. In 1891-92, his first full season with the club, he was the leading scorer with 17 goals in 25 games including another hat-trick in a 9-0 rout of Darwen. In April 1896, he netted his third hat-trick and the first by a Burnley player in an East Lancashire Derby as the Clarets beat Blackburn Rovers 6-0. He had scored 44 goals in 149 games when in December 1896 he joined rivals Blackburn Rovers. After just one season at Ewood Park, he moved to Southampton where after being switched to full-back, he ended his playing days.

Peter Noble (Burnley)

Peter Noble began his league career with Newcastle United before joining Swindon Town in January 1968. During his time at the County Ground, Noble helped the Robins win the League Cup and the Third Division Championship before in May 1973, joining Burnley for £40,000. One of the most popular Clarets players of all-time, he netted four hat-tricks for the club, his first coming in a 4-1 defeat over his former club Newcastle United. He had scored 80 goals in 300 League and Cup games of which 18 were penalties before he was prematurely sold to Blackpool for £25,000. He never really settled at Bloomfield Road and in

May 1983 decided to hang up his boots after being released by the Seasiders.

Louis Page (Burnley)

Louis Page had spells with Stoke and Northampton before arriving at Turf Moor, ending his first season, 1925-26 as the club's top scorer with 26 goals in 41 game. Included in that total was a hat-trick against Leeds United and six goals in a 7-1 win at Birmingham, the first time he'd played centre-forward. Forming a formidable strike force with George Beel, his goalscoring feats were rewarded with selection for England at full international level. He had scored 115 goals in 259 games for Burnley when in March 1932 he left to play for Manchester United. Unable to settle at Old Trafford, he had a spell with Port Vale before becoming player-manager of Yeovil Town. He later managed Newport County, Swindon Town and Chester.

Walter Place Senior (Burnley)

Known as 'Big Walter', he first appeared in the Burnley side in 1886 when he was just 16-years-old. However, he then left to play for Colne and Bacup before rejoining the Clarets for the start of the 1890-91 season. Place wore almost every outfield shirt for the Clarets and because of injury to Jack Hillman, started two games in goal! Walter Place, who scored nine goals in 149 League and Cup games, was a great all-round sportsman, for not only was he more than capable of holding his own at bowls, cricket and snooker, he was also recognised as the country's best wrestler following an international tournament at Blackburn.

Bob Pryde (Blackburn Rovers)

Bob Pryde began his career with St Johnstone but following a loan spell with Brechin City, he joined Blackburn Rovers in the summer of 1933. After playing his early games at left-half, he settled down into the centre-half position. A dominant force at the heart of the Rovers defence, he helped the club to their Second Division Championship in 1938-39 and though he lost the best years of his career to the Second World War, he was still the club's first-choice pivot when the game resumed in 1946-47. After three more seasons in which he took his total of League and Cup appearances to 345 and 11 goals, he left Ewood Park to become player-manager of then non-League Wigan Athletic.

Len Smelt (Burnley)

After playing his early football for Gainsborough Trinity, Len Smelt 'guested' for Rotherham County, Leeds City and Burnley before joining the Clarets on a permanent basis in March 1919.

In 1919-20 his first season with the club, he was ever-present as Burnley ended the campaign as runners-up in the First Division. The following season he helped the Clarets win the League Championship. Over the next four seasons, he missed very few matches and on 17 November 1923, his 100th consecutive match for the club, he captained them to a 5-1 victory over West Ham United. After appearing in 248 League and Cup games for Burnley, he coached the club's youngsters before leaving to end his playing career with Barrow.

Jack Southworth (Blackburn Rovers)

Blackburn Rovers' first prolific goalscorer, Jack Southworth injured his right knee whilst 'guesting' for Accrington and so on his return to Blackburn Olympic, turned his hand to goalkeeping. He helped them beat Rovers in the final of the Lancashire Cup before leaving to work as a musician in a Chester theatre. Having overcome his injury problems, he returned to Blackburn and on joining the Rovers, resumed his old position of centre-forward. He captained the side in the club's first season of League football, netting a hat-trick in Rovers first league meeting with Burnley at Turf Moor, a match the Clarets lost 7-1. Capped three times by England, he won two FA Cup winners' medals with Rovers and had scored 122 goals in 133 games before ending his career with Everton.

Nat Walton (Blackburn Rovers)

Along with William Townley, Nat Walton combined to make one of Rovers first really successful left-wing partnerships. The industrious inside-forward was left out of the club's 1885 FA Cup Final side as they decided to play three half-backs. However, twelve months later he won an FA Cup winners' medal as Rovers beat West Bromwich Albion 2-0 after a goalless draw and won two more in 1890 and 1891. An England international, ageing legs slowed him down and after losing his place in the side, he switched positions to become the club's first-choice goalkeeper!

Walton, who scored 49 goals in 139 games, later played for Nelson before returning to take up his original trade of coach builder.

Arnold Whiteside (Blackburn Rovers)

A weaver by trade, Arnold Whiteside left the mill where he worked at Calder Vale to join Blackburn Rovers in 1932. After some impressive performances in the club's Central League side, he established himself at half-back in Rovers' first team. At one stage, his Ewood Park career seemed over, for with the club languishing at the foot of the Second Division, he was transfer listed. Surprisingly the club received no offers and after Bob Crompton re-signed him, he helped Rovers win the Second Division Championship in 1938-39. He continued to turn out for the club during the hostilities and in 1940 helped them win the War Cup Final. After the war, he took his total of first team appearances in which he scored three goals to 239 before being released.

Arthur Woodruff (Burnley)

The oldest player to appear in League football for the Clarets since the Second World War, Arthur Woodruff joined Burnley from Bradford City in the summer of 1936. A virtual ever-present in the three seasons leading up to the outbreak of the Second World War, he was still a member of the Burnley side when league football resumed in 1946-47. In that season he helped the club win promotion to the top flight and appeared for Burnley in the FA Cup Final where they were beaten 1-0 by Charlton Athletic. His performances led to him playing representative football for the Football League but in 1952, he left Turf Moor, having played in 292 League and Cup games to join Workington.

Matt Woods (Blackburn Rovers)

Blackburn manager Johnny Carey paid Everton 6,000 to bring centre-half Matt Woods to Ewood Park in November 1956. Playing between Ronnie Clayton and Mick McGrath, Woods helped to form one of the best half-back lines in the club's history. He was ever-present in 1957-58 when Rovers won promotion to the First Division and won an FA Cup runners-up medal in 1960. Although he played for the Football League, he never won full international honours. Having played in 307 League and Cup games for Rovers, he emigrated to Australia to play for Hakoah and later captained the Australian national team. On his return to these shores, he played for Luton Town and Stockport County, helping the Cheshire club win the Fourth Division Championship.

Statistics

Blackburn Rovers

	P.	W.	D.	L.	F.	A.
Football League	82	36	13	33	156	141
Test Matches	2	0	0	2	1	5
FA Cup	5	2	1	2	9	7
Anglo-Scottish Cup	4	0	3	1	5	6
Manx Cup	5	3	1	1	8	4
Wartime Matches	37	13	7	17	61	77
TOTAL	**135**	**54**	**25**	**56**	**240**	**240**

Burnley

	F.	W.	D.	L.	F.	A.
Football League	82	33	13	36	141	156
Test Matches	2	2	0	0	5	1
FA Cup	5	2	1	2	7	9
Anglo-Scottish Cup	4	1	3	0	6	5
Manx Cup	5	1	1	3	4	8
Wartime Matches	37	17	7	13	77	61
TOTAL	**135**	**56**	**25**	**54**	**240**	**240**

Biggest Wins

Blackburn Rovers

Home	Away
7-1 in 1889-90	7-1 in 1888-89
6-0 in 1914-15	

Burnley

Home	Away
6-0 in 1895-96	5-1 in 1926-27

Highest Aggregate Score

Blackburn Rovers 8 Burnley 3 at Ewood Park 1929-30.

Most Appearances (League and Cup)

		League	Cup	Total
1=	Jerrey Dawson (Burnley)	18	1	19
	Ronnie Clayton (Blackburn. R)	15	4	19
3=	John Angus (Burnley)	15	2	17
	Bryan Douglas (Blackburn. R)	14	3	17
5=	Adam Blacklaw (Burnley)	14	2	16
	Brian Miller (Burnley)	13	3	16
	Billy Bowes	16	0	16
8.	Tom Brandon (Blackburn. R)	15	0	15
9=	Mick McGrath (Blackburn. R)	11	3	14
	Tom McLintock (Burnley)	14	0	14
	Walter Place snr (Burnley)	14	0	14
	Billy Watson (Burnley)	14	0	14

Note: Bob Brocklebank, Arthur Woodruff and Tom Gardner of Burnley and Bob Pryde of Blackburn Rovers, all appeared in 27 East Lancashire Derby games but the majority of their appearances were in wartime games

Most Goals

		League	Cup	Total
1.	Jack Southworth (Blackburn. R)	12	0	12
2.	Nat Walton (Blackburn. R)	9	0	9
3.	Percy Dawson (Blackburn. R)	8	0	8
4=	Ben Cross (Burnley)	6	0	6
	Bob Kelly (Burnley)	6	0	6
	Andy McCluggage (Burnley)	6	0	6
	Tom McLean (Blackburn. R)	6	0	6
	Louis Page (Burnley)	6	0	6
9=	Joe Anderson (Burnley)	5	0	5
	John Connelly (Burnley)	4	1	5
	Peter Dobing (Blackburn. R)	2	3	5
	Ted Harper (Blackburn. R)	5	0	5
	John McIntyre (Blackburn. R)	5	0	5
	Tom Nicol (Burnley)	5	0	5
	Syd Puddefoot (Blackburn. R)	5	0	5
	William Townley (Blackburn. R)	5	0	5

Four Goals in a Match

Percy Dawson (Blackburn. R) in 1914-15
Bob Brocklebank (Burnley) in 1943-44 (Wartime)
Cecil Wyles (Blackburn. R) in 1945-46 (Wartime)

Hat-Tricks

Jack Southworth (Blackburn. R) in 1888-89

Tom Nicol (Burnley) in 1895-96

Wilf Toman (Burnley) in 1897-98 (Test Matches)

Bert Freeman (Burnley) in 1917-18 (Wartime)

Bert Freeman (Burnley) in 1918-19 (Wartime)

John McIntyre (Blackburn. R) in 1924-25

Ted Harper (Blackburn. R) in 1925-26

Arthur Rigby (Blackburn. R) in 1925-26

Albert Groves (Blackburn. R) in 1929-30

Highest Attendances

1.	53,839 at Ewood Park	1960
2.	52,920 at Ewood Park	1952
3.	51,501 at Turf Moor	1960
4.	48,000 at Ewood Park	1914
5.	44,240 at Turf Moor	1948
6.	43,752 at Ewood Park	1959
7.	43,000 at Ewood Park	1921
8.	42,778 at Ewood Park	1913
9.	42,289 at Ewood Park	1926
10.	41,961 at Turf Moor	1958

Select Bibliography

Blackburn Rovers – A Complete Record by Mike Jackman

Blackburn Rovers, An A-Z by Dean Hayes

The Blue and Whites by Dean Hayes

Burnley FC – A Complete Record by Edward Lee and Ray Simpson

Burnley FC – A Pictorial History of the Clarets by Tony Durkin

Up the Clarets by David Wiseman

Burnley FC, An A-Z by Dean Hayes

Blackburn Rovers and Burnley club programmes

Derby days, past and present ...

Turf Moor: Burnley F.C.'s ground — scene of many derbies

Match 104, 16 March, 1960

Match 118, 27 December, 1976:
Burnley's Ian Brennan fires home a late equaliser in the 2-2 draw with Rovers.

Match 119, 8 April, 1977: Burnley's third goal is scored by the 19-year-old
centre-half Peter Robinson who curls his header over the stranded Paul Bradshaw.

Match 119, 8 April 1977: Rovers' keeper Paul Bradshaw is beaten but Malcolm Smith's shot flies narrowly wide.

Match 119, 8 April, 1977: Paul Bradshaw plucks the ball off the head of Burnley striker Paul Fletcher as the Clarets threaten the Rovers' goal.

Match 121, 26 December 1977: Peter Noble beats John Butcher from the penalty-spot and though the referee added on seven minutes injury-time, the Clarets couldn't force an equaliser.

Match 122, 27 March, 1978: Despite John Butcher's despairing dive, he can do nothing to prevent Burnley's Terry Cochrane scoring the only goal of the game from fully 25 yards.

Match 122, 27 March, 1978: Blackburn Rover's Northern Ireland international winger Noel Brotherston is sent off by referee George Courtney after he had brought down Terry Cochrane.

Match 124, 26 December, 1978: Steve Kindon, who had just been penalised for a foul on John Waddington, suddenly collapsed in a heap. Here Brian Miller remonstrates with the referee, who delayed the Burnley trainer's entrance on to the field of play.

Match 125, 14 April, 1979: Former Liverpool midfielder Brian Hall scores the Clarets' second goal in a 2-1 win at Ewood Park.

Match 127, 27 December, 1982: Colin Randell looks on as Terry Gennoe is hit on the head by a coin thrown from the crowd.

Match 128, 4 April, 1983: Burnley's Northern Ireland international centre-forward Billy Hamilton beats David Mail to the ball as the Clarets go in search of an equaliser.

Match 128, 4 April, 1983: Derek Scott pulls a goal back for Burnley, firing past a static Terry Gennoe.

Players, 1888-2001

November, 1888:
Jimmy Forrest
(Blackburn Rovers)

November, 1888:
Jack Southworth
(Blackburn Rovers)

February, 1890:
William Townley
(Blackburn Rovers)

November, 1890:
Nat Walton
(Blackburn Rovers)

December 1891:
Herbie Arthur
(Blackburn Rovers' keeper)

Match 29, 3 April, 1915:
Eddie Latherton
(Blackburn Rovers)

1919 - 41: Bob Crompton
(Blackburn Rovers)

1933 - 47: Tom Brandon
(Blackburn Rovers)

1950s - 60s: Jimmy McIlroy (Burnley)

1955 - 60: Ronnie Clayton (Blackburn
Rovers)

1958: Harry Leyland (Blackburn Rovers)

1956 - Matt Woods
(Blackburn Rovers)

March, 1960: Jimmy Robson (Burnley)

January, 1959:
Bill Eckersley (Blackburn Rovers)

October, 1959:
Roy Vernon (Blackburn Rovers)

October, 1962:
Fred Else (Blackburn Rovers)

February, 1965:
Mike England (Blackburn Rovers)

January, 1966: Brian Flynn (Burnley)

1973 - 83: Peter Noble (Burnley)

April, 1983: Burnley captain Martin Dobson appeals for calm from the Clarets fans
during the 16-minute stoppage of the East Lancashire Derby.

1980s: Simon Garner (right)
(Blackburn Rovers)

April, 2001: John Angus (Burnley)

More Lancashire books from Sigma Leisure:

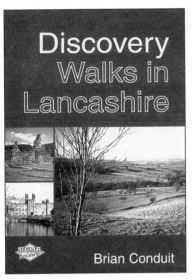

DISCOVERY WALKS IN LANCASHIRE
Brian Conduit
Walks with a heritage theme: Roman remains, medieval castles and abbeys, nature reserves, country parks and (of course) the many monuments to the county's role in the industrial revolution. "An impressive variety of walks...rounded off with some fascinating details on interesting features" BLACKPOOL GAZETTE. £6.95

WALKS IN MYSTERIOUS LANCASHIRE
Graham Dugdale
Delving into a host of mysterious places throughout Lancashire, this unusual collection of 30 walks, suitable for all the family, will appeal to walkers with enquiring minds. From the enchanting follies of Lord Levenshulme of Bivington to the origins of the 'American Dream' in Worton, history and legend are inextricably linked in this succession of fine walks set in the superb Lancashire landscape. Lucid walking directions and the author's ornate, hand-drawn maps complement the entertaining commentary. £6.95

50 CLASSIC WALKS IN LANCASHRE
Terry Marsh
"The walking country of Lancashire ranks amongst the finest in the British Isles" says Terry Marsh, who writes with the determined aim of enlightening those whose image of the county is unfavourable. He reveals Lancashire at its diverse best - from wild woodland expanses and witch country, to tranquil river valleys. £7.95

BY-WAY BIKING IN LANCASHIRE
Henry Tindell
From Morecambe Bay to Bolton and from Blackpool to Burnley, Henry Tindell reveals Lancashire's outstanding potential as a destination for mountain bikers.
"A fine variety of off-road tracks lead you to a wealth of countryside and villages all within easy reach of the large northern towns and cities". BOLTON ADVERTISER. £7.95

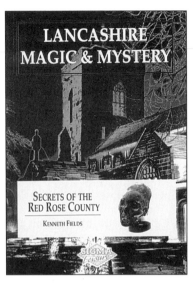

LANCASHIRE MAGIC & MYSTERY: Secrets of the Red Rose County
Kenneth Fields
Covering all of Lancashire, including Merseyside and Greater Manchester, Ken Field's book guides you to places of mystery and curiosity. With tales of hauntings, witchcraft, religious relics, folklore and UFOs, this is a must for anyone interested in the supernatural. £6.95

CHILLING TRUE TALES OF OLD LANCASHIRE
Keith Johnson
Set in Victorian Lancashire, here is a spine-chilling collection of tales - "...sure to thrill, chill and amaze" THE LANCASTER GUARDIAN. £6.95

WHERE TO FISH - Lancashire Coarse Fisheries
Martin Salisbury
Endorsed by Martin James, presenter of BBC Radio Lancashire's "From the Water's Edge", this is the definitive guide to angling in Lancashire, covering 113 fisheries with details of stillwaters, rivers and canals. £6.95

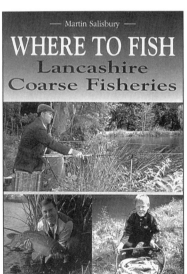

CATHERINE ROTHWELL'S LANCASHIRE COOKBOOK
There are 180 recipes in total for you to try, ranging from early simple traditional cookery to more sophisticated contemporary dishes - all arranged in a logical, easy-to-use format. Recipes are fully tested. £6.95

TOWN AND VILLAGES OF BRITAIN: LANCASHIRE
Michael Smout
The moors, valleys and mossland of Lancashire are the backdrop to this account of the county's towns and villages. "The histories of our towns and villages neatly gathered in one definitive guide" SOUTHPORT VISITER. £8.95

Our books are all available through booksellers. In case of difficulty, or for a free catalogue, please contact:
SIGMA LEISURE, 1 SOUTH OAK LANE, WILMSLOW, CHESHIRE SK9 6AR.
Phone: 01625-531035   Fax: 01625-536800. E-mail: info@sigmapress.co.uk
Web site: http//www.sigmapress.co.uk

MASTERCARD and VISA orders welcome.